AMERICAN THEATRE IN THE TWENTY-FIRST CENTURY

ABSURD, SYMBOLIC & POETIC

SHORT PLAYS

ISBN: 978-1-953818-34-8
Library of Congress Control Number: 2020922358

  Publisher's Cataloging-in-Publication Data

American Theatre in the Twenty-First Century: absurd, symbolic & poetic short plays / Future Publishing House Anthology Series, edited by Shaun Vain.

    214 p.

    Includes index.

    ISBN   978-1-953818-32-4   (pb)   978-1-953818-34-8   (hc) 978-1-953818-30-0   (ebook   1)   978-1-953818-31-7   (ebook   2) 978-1-953818-33-1 (ebook 3)

1. Drama—21st Century. 2. Literature—Collections. I. Title. II. Series Name. III. Editor.

PN6110.5-A.44 V.35 2020

812.54 ddc   LCCN: 2020922358

10 9 8 7 6   FPH   e 4 3 2 1
12 06 24 23 22 21 20
First edition.

Cover design by Kiirstn Pagan. FPH logo design by Mary Parrish.

THIS IS A FUTURE PUBLISHING HOUSE ANTHOLOGY
BALTIMORE, MARYLAND

TABLE OF CONTENTS

A
FUTURE PUBLISHING HOUSE
ANTHOLOGY

Volume 1:
Theatre

Introduction

Setting the scene for several plays, this anthology encapsulates the thoughts of playwrights living in this century who live, work, and play in the real world. Even though some plays may be abstract, society and the forces that move us root themselves within this text. Such a pervasive reflection is needed in order to achieve harmony. Social mechanisms, which provide employment, welfare, buildings, and all other aspects of humanity, often minimize the value of art. Ruthlessly, the playwright offers a voice built on natural rhythm, and the product, as it is often found within literature, is a sophisticated reflection of society. Playwrights, as artists, may promote ideals important to shaping and reshaping the world, or they may choose to offer an entertaining spectacle.

The reason that theatre folk discuss the same dramatic works written long ago is because those plays were once powerful and provocative. Twenty-first century theatre is written for twenty-first century people, yet the selections here possess a similar capacity to provoke, resulting in a universal quality. Preserving plays in such a form adds to the scenes and monologues of which theatre artists are consistently using to break through the veil of ordinary life. Thus, humanity learns new perspectives on issues that would otherwise plague the human condition.

Despite the notion of American culture melting together (or melting away, as exemplified in the twentieth century play *The Melting Pot* by Israel Zangwill), it's crucial to learn backgrounds of playwrights to gain context for their work. Of those who are willing to share, playwrights whose works are featured in this collection claim Irish, Polish, Welsh, French, English, Italian, Croatian, Scottish, Jewish, Czechoslovakian, Dutch, and Swiss backgrounds.

Even though the backgrounds of playwrights hardly compare to the abundance of culture within the Americas—of which the largest groups in the United States are German, Irish, Black/ African American (non-Hispanic), and English[1]—the details within their work provide a more accurate depiction of the people living in America. For example, *Chalked* features a cast of white and black characters, and other roles are open to multiple races. One of the playwrights in this anthology commented, "*Chalked* has great dynamics among the characters and language that effectively captures a range of perspectives." Such intention, to provide roles for people of all backgrounds, is scattered within the plays, throughout this anthology. Many of the roles are flexible to all types of casting choices.

On Short Plays

While theatre enthusiasts may typically require caffeine or a cozy nook to get through reading a full-length stage play, short plays require far less commitment. They're easy to read aloud with your friends and family, and they're incredibly feasible to produce on a modest budget. (See page 199 for guidance on obtaining performance rights.)

Short plays are easy to finish reading in one sitting; strong conflicts emerge to thrill the audience, and sharp conclusions relieve the most impatient spectator. Short plays send one into a dream-like state consisting of uninterrupted stimulation for one's imagination. In order for a reader to be truly encapsulated by the suspension of disbelief, which theatrical works rely heavily upon, it's helpful to read plays from start to finish without breaking away from the experience. Devote yourself to getting lost in the spirit of live performance.

If you're someone who needs to properly adjust your temperament to accept theatrical works that are presented in print, perhaps you could recall why it is that people appreciate theatre in the first place. Consider how Broadway represents the pinnacle of American drama since the beginning of the twentieth-century, yet there's an undeniable relevance obtained in fringe theatre. While it's impressive to witness a show with large budgets for performers, costumes, set designs, et cetera, these types of shows are wrought with spectacle. Often times, meaningful messages that were originally intended for audiences become muddled with complications. Broadening your horizon, particularly to the fringe of theatre, is one way to discover the cusp of new ideas and concepts. Such newness will shake up the regular pace of theatre goers and readers alike.

It's no coincidence that playwrights in this anthology have found cozy homes for their theatrical works at fringe theatre festivals. For instance, Alexander Scally's one-man show at Charm City Fringe Festival, Barbara Bryan's *Leaving the Universe* at Black Dog Theatre Festival, and John Enright's romantic comedy, *O'Brien & O'Brian*, at the New York International Fringe Festival.

As a lighting designer and technician for an original cabaret show by Bremner Duthie, I've seen the fringe up close. As a venue manager, I've seen dilapidated buildings, which were once bustling centers of commerce, serve as incredibly unique performance venues. I've seen what fringe events do to a city. During Charm City Fringe's 2017 festival, what once was a training center for pharmacy employees turned into a venue for dozens of performers over the span of a few short weeks.

Furthermore, well-orchestrated fringe theatre festivals will revive crumbling buildings and enliven arts districts for entire communities. "That might be the biggest sign we've had so far of our success in building a community is activating those two blocks, [300 and 400 blocks of Howard Street,] this past year," said Zachary Michel, co-founder of Charm City Fringe. "It was the first time we had a visible and substantive step towards a vibrant theatre ground. Those blocks were vacant, largely. And had little to no businesses occupying them."[2]

Michael Brush, the other co-founder of Charm City Fringe, made claims of the company's artistic support: "There's a lot of really great theatre that's happening here. We just want to continue to see it grow. Our thought has always been that the more theatre you put into the community, the higher you are going to raise that bar."

Playwrights all around the country develop new work on their own volition, yet some pieces grow through support from established programs. Melanie Coffey and Emma S. Rund are members of the Chicago Dramatists, a thriving community with the mission of "nurturing dramatic writers" through providing classes, scholarships, fundraising, and other opportunities for growth. Rund and Cameron Sheppard are members of Chicago's Women's Theatre Alliance; the mission of this non-profit is to provide "a union of theatre artists (of all genders) and theatre organizations which support all women, female identifying and gender non-binary individuals." The amount of outside influence required to shape short plays found in this anthology is certainly extraordinary.

Before I set forth the most diplomatic critique of this collection, I'd like to mention what a joy these plays have brought to the lives of those involved in this project, even from the detached editorial perspective. It's a great honor to bring together this anthology with those who worked hard on each piece of it, including designers, editors, librarians, scholars, professors, dramaturges, actors, playwrights, and everyone who caught a glimpse of this project being developed.

With the help of peer reviews from a committee of theatre artists, teachers, analysts, and writers, our selection was narrowed down to the twelve plays bound within this anthology. Thanks to Denise T. Smolarek, Jessica Ruth Baker, Katherine Kopajtic, Kenny Leon Horning, Benjamin Robb, and Alex Calvin for their efforts involved in reading through submissions. The review committee worked behind the scenes, and they played an integral role in the foundation of this book. Special thanks to Jessica and Denise for directing vignettes of plays featured in this anthology.

Our review committee read plays without author names attached, maintaining an authentic selection process. They weighed in on their favorite plays for this anthology, and they selected the plays you're about to read. This book would not have been possible without their friendly support and camaraderie. They were also given the option to flag inappropriate material. (See page 10 of this introduction for a list of plays with coarse language and adult themes.)

Curatorial Remarks

One of the many pleasures involved in compiling an anthology of works, which were delicately crafted by the hands and minds of twentieth-century playwrights, is in choosing an order for which the plays are to appear. For genre-specific information, themes, and topics, make sure to flip through the index.

Although readers may dive into these plays on their own volition, without preconceived expectations, this section supplies information to help with understanding why these plays are presented in print. Furthermore, you may realize the authors' intentions behind writing for the stage.

Including insights from a review committee and third-party reviewers, there are many creative individuals behind this anthology project. "The personality of the artist passes into the narrative itself, flowing round and round the persons and the action like a vital sea," wrote James Joyce (*A Portrait of the Artist as a Young Man*). "The dramatic form is reached when the vitality which has flowed and eddied round each person fills every person with such vital force that he or she assumes a proper and intangible esthetic life." In order to properly introduce these plays, a few particularly notable individuals will be introduced to give additional perspectives.

Dereck Stafford Mangus, Baltimore-based artist and writer (*Artblog*, *frieze* magazine, *Full Bleed*), reviewed *American Theatre in the Twenty-First Century*, making the following remarks:

> Considering the ongoing war on reason and following the many confounding events of 2020, absurdist theater is newly ascendant. Its trajectory is amply affirmed in this compelling new anthology, which offers numerous examples of absurdist themes updated for the twenty-first century. Albert Camus advised us to embrace the absurd condition of human existence. To better cope with our increasingly peculiar world, I advise you to read (and perform!) these plays.

This collection starts off with a play by Melanie Coffey. Unlike Coffey's second play in this anthology, *To You & Me & the Ocean* isn't concerned with direct community involvement in political decision making. This play focuses on the lives of people impacted by climate change. Mangus offers the following critique of this first piece:

> Through a sparse and tight use of dialogue, [Coffey] evokes a poignant if fleeting scene of female camaraderie. Despite its ambiguous setting, the vignette aptly conveys a sense of dread and even doom. What's happening? Is the world ending? Yet, it's the friends' love for each other that is the main point of the play. It's through their exchange, through their words that we feel their connection. In these end-of-days times, it's within these lingering pockets of love and nostalgia that we retain our humanity.

Following Coffey's imaginative play is an equally creative dip into surrealism. Barbara Bryan's short play *Leaving the Universe* could be characterized as a quick-witted, symbolic metaphor for change. The symbolism of everything-must-go yard sales works in conjunction with inspirations from the playwright's travels in New Mexico. *Leaving the Universe* is humorous, its characters are strange, and its plethora of props offer seemingly unlimited options for theatre artists.

A scene from Cameron Sheppard's full-length play entitled *Mary Doesn't Wear Red Lipstick* is one of the most autobiographical pieces to be featured in this collection. Readers see into the soul of a young person overcome with a search for her own identity. Sheppard's play has subtle imagery, heightened realism, religious symbolism, and hypnotic dialogue. The action of this scene entices the reader with a memorable, vivid hallucination, as experienced by the play's protagonist.

Emma S. Rund's *To Fix A Dinosaur* is a fast-paced dramatic work. Through clever use of props and costume, this play is a reminder of the painful moments of life, which may happen to any one of us. Rund's lesson is plain to see, but it's one of the most important things to learn: we are not alone through tragic moments. *To Fix A Dinosaur* was a favorite of more than one person from our review committee; this play was unanimously selected by each member of the committee, perhaps due to its convincing metaphors and subtle imagery.

Moving into a classical poetic piece, *Iago's Deal* by John Joseph Enright hovers in the realm of creative geniuses. This play is a stark contrast to whimsical, amusing work by Enright, featured later in this anthology. Enright's range as a playwright is apparent. In this continuation of Shakespeare's *Othello, the Moor of Venice*, Enright's craftsmanship rings true in rhyme, meter, and masterful use of English poetic verse. *Iago's Deal* answers questions that Shakespeare left for us to ponder, questions scholars have been asking for hundreds of years.

The first play by Alexander Scally to be included in this anthology is entitled *Chalked*. Of this play, Mangus writes:

> This short play is a 'slice of life' on the surface, but simmers with a darkness seething quite literally underfoot. What appears to be a simple vignette about urban life in Baltimore, surreptitiously expands to encompass socio-economic commentary about white

flight and gentrification, culminating with a poetic observation by the main character, Leonard, a mainstay of the neighborhood. In a few terse lines, we move from quotidian scene to critical exposition to, ultimately, poetry.

This piece is brutal, dramatic, and poignant in how it shows a neighborhood accustomed to destruction.

Alexander Scally's *Cake Day* is another example of a playwright's ability to write a wide range of material. *Cake Day* is a piece that's far more playful, yet there's a sinister undertone reminiscent of Scally's other piece. *Cake Day* explores unusual social constructs in a familiar office setting. Witness what happens when a common social event is taken to a new level. With each line, mundane customs become increasingly absurd.

The next piece, *Party Planet* by Dylan Kinnett, relies heavily on physical prowess of actors, maneuvering in a faux outer space set. This strange, futuristic dark comedy is a proper juxtaposition to Kinnett's other play in this anthology, which relies heavily upon wordplay. In addition to an eerie setting and theme, *Party Planet* provides a satirical critique of the future of humanity as we grapple with our own technological creations.

Easy as Pie by Melanie Coffey follows with drama of a strong political variety. This play shows just how far people will go to make change in society, particularly when political leaders have distasteful beliefs and policies. *Easy as Pie* arrives at a time when similar coups are far from fictional. However, this unique piece explores what would happen if women's liberation movements operate under extremist dogma.

While both of Kinnett's plays implement wit and precision to build notable archetypal characters, *The Piece of Real Estate at the Top of the Tallest Building on Earth* is, in essence, a mouthful of the current trends in society. Particularly, Kinnett confronts his readers with constant competitive dealings of a growing business. Though, there are symbols at play for something grander. This play's lengthy title is an entertaining phrase that actors must say a total of four times throughout the piece. You'll notice the way Kinnett's dialogue snaps into place before your eyes, much like the race for the next, tall high-rise.

Love, Lust, Lyrics & Stamps is the only work in this collection to be co-authored by more than one playwright. Matt Brown and Andre Thespies put this play together years before the US Post Office was declared an endangered government entity. This tragic, satiric melodrama is a harsh criticism of human nature when action is fueled by emotion. The dark motives of an anti-hero protagonist postal employee are overshadowed by Brown's dry humor.

Rounding off this collection is John Joseph Enright's *Starry Night*. Kimberly Exum, who plays the role of Nabulungi in *The Book of Mormon* on Broadway, provides the following reaction: "What a fun play—The curiosity, combined with political commentary, and sci-fi elements reminded me of a quirky, lost *Twilight Zone* episode." This entertaining short play makes one wonder about whether life may exist beyond the planet that is our home. In a time when technology is steadily improving its reach, will aliens be the ones to initiate contact with humanity? Exum, who writes in-depth reports for an industry news source called *Broadway Black*, also adds, "[*Starry Night*] forced me to look at our world from the outside in. A perfect capsule for a post-Trump America."

In order to facilitate those adapting these plays to the stage and for the benefit of readers, the following information was prepared. These plays have coarse language and/or adult themes: *Mary Doesn't Wear Red Lipstick*; *To Fix A Dinosaur*; *Chalked*; *Easy as Pie*; *Party Planet*; *The Piece of Real Estate at the Top of the Tallest Building on Earth*; and *Love, Lust, Lyrics & Stamps*.

WHERE THEATRE IS GOING

This anthology project provides a glimpse of hope for playwrights and theatre professionals, concerning the remainder of the century and of America. If an independent publisher is able to connect people, who are separated by thousands of miles, in a matter of months, to build this anthology, others will follow.

For the folks behind the scenes at Future Publishing House, this anthology is the first in a series of three distinct forms of literature. This publication serves to encourage small publishers, artist collectives, and writers of all sorts. While our company is able to facilitate the means of publication for a select few playwrights (short story authors in the second volume and poets in the third volume), the means of publishing a powerful, provocative, creative piece of literature are well within your reach. For those who need assistance finding a path to publishing and producing new work, don't lose hope.

The inspiration that comes from working on collaborative projects is unbelievable. Our playwrights were brave enough to share their creations. Reviewers were equipped with knowledge of theatre and the desire to contribute to growing this project. There isn't a way for me to express the depth of enjoyment we have for this work without recalling our first read of these plays.

While sitting in a café with creative consultant Julia Golonka, I had an opportunity to listen to the heartbeat of live theatre. Meanwhile, an art-school graduate with a background in filmmaking wondered whether these plays are conceivable. Consider this the passing of a torch from those who worked on creating this anthology, to you and whichever stage is fit for you to take.

Shaun Vain, editor

---

[1] U.S. Census Bureau, Ancestry: 2000, issued June 2004; 2015 American Community Survey.

[2] Behind the Mask: Michael Brush and Zachary Michel (Full Report), issued February 2018; the Mid-Atlantic Exposé.

To You & Me & the Ocean

by Melanie Coffey

Cast of Characters:

Saoirse, she/her/hers, being sent to California
Lore, she/her/hers, a scientist, staying behind

Setting:

Beside the ocean, steps leading into the water, America

Time:

The future, the consequences of climate change are happening

Additional Notes:

"/" means the next characters say their line overlapping with the currently speaking character.

Keep it calm, soft, slow, this is their last moment together, it's nostalgic.

SCENE: On a set of concrete steps down into the ocean, we hear the waves crash against them throughout the conversation. LORE and SAOIRSE, sit on a step, legs dangling into the water, a bottle of ouzo between them, sipping from tea cups.

LORE: I've been going through all of the old photos, how were we ever that happy? Smiling faces, sunshine that didn't burn, pretty dresses and coffee cups with lipstick stains. The luxury of having lips uncovered in a public place.

SAOIRSE: I know.

LORE: (*hates to say it out-loud*) I miss it.

SAOIRSE: You can't. Don't. Don't think about it.

LORE: Yeah.

SAOIRSE: What does your mother always say?

LORE: These days? Nothing.

SAOIRSE: Hey.

LORE: "Be happy for what we have, others have less."

SAOIRSE: Exactly.

LORE: I still miss it.

SAOIRSE: What do we have? Right now, what do we have?

LORE: Tea cups and ouzo. Each other. The beach.

SAOIRSE: All good things.

LORE: (*lifting her cup*) A toast!

SAOIRSE: To what?

LORE: To you and me and the ocean.

SAOIRSE: Hear, hear! It will all be missed!

LORE: How much time do we have?

SAOIRSE: I don't know.

LORE: Check.

SAOIRSE: I don't want to know. (*holds up her tea cup*) To you, Lore, a true legend.

LORE: I see what you did there.

SAOIRSE: I thought you would.

LORE: To you, Saoirse: such good luck in California. I'm gonna miss you like crazy.

SAOIRSE: You'll come and visit.

LORE: You're drunk.

SAOIRSE: I'm not drunk, I'm...sparkly.

LORE: Tipsy?

SAOIRSE: I've heard it both ways. You'll visit, right?

LORE: Do they still let you get on planes drunk? (*off of Saoirse's reaction*) I haven't been on a plane in years, not since the requirements, I don't know what you can and can't do.

SAOIRSE: You can still drink on planes they kinda prefer it, I've heard. Makes the turbulence over the middle lands a bit easier to get through.

LORE: Right.

(*Beat.*)

SAOIRSE: Lore.

LORE: Yes?

SAOIRSE: You'll visit me?

LORE: I don't see how I can.

SAOIRSE: But—

LORE: I can't fly. I didn't pass standards. And trains are too expensive, going around the midlands...it's too dangerous these days.

SAOIRSE: You could—

LORE: What? Bike? Bike to California?

SAOIRSE: No.

LORE: Well then.

SAOIRSE: Yeah, well then.

LORE: Sorry.

SAOIRSE: So I guess I /should—

LORE: I guess we should change the subject.

SAOIRSE: Wow.

LORE: We don't have time to talk about dark things.

SAOIRSE: I thought we didn't know what time it is.

LORE: Judging from the sun, we don't have time to fill
with dark things.

> (*LORE hops down from the step, down to the further one, feet
> in the water, pushes the water around.*)

LORE: I heard that Pip got into the program. The
island program.

SAOIRSE: Really? That's disgusting.

LORE: Is it? She'll be safe.

SAOIRSE: She'll be used. It's not an equal transaction.

LORE: But she'll be safe on an island, fed, have access to clean water.

SAOIRSE: Having babies as payment for being kept safe is never okay. It should never be something that can be justified.

LORE: No, I know. But she won't be called up to California.

SAOIRSE: (*quietly*) Yeah. Well good for her.

LORE: So she'll leave and you'll leave and it'll be me and the ocean.

SAOIRSE: This isn't happy.

LORE: No. You're right. Sorry.

SAOIRSE: Remember when we used to go crabbing over there on the rocks? When we were kids?

LORE: Never caught anything.

SAOIRSE: That wasn't really the point.

LORE: My mom would say differently.

SAOIRSE: Or we'd swim out with books and bake in the sun and read.

LORE: Until someone found us.

SAOIRSE: Hide the books in the crevices. With the crabs.

Or I guess not.

LORE: I can't imagine not living near the water. It's like an old friend. I swear it tells me how to feel.

SAOIRSE: I know. Calming, thrilling.

LORE: You'll have the Pacific.

SAOIRSE: No swimming though.

LORE: True.

   (*Pause.*)

LORE: (*continuing*) But still it's a constant, with tides that pull you to it, reminding you that you belong. Belong somewhere.

SAOIRSE: You gonna be okay?

LORE: (*watches SAOIRSE, hesitates*) I...can't complain.

   (*SAOIRSE gets the hint. The hint? SAOIRSE is going to have it much worse.*

   LORE raises her cup.)

LORE: To all of the days we spent getting drunk on the rock island, swimming out with bags of contraband—

SAOIRSE: And drinking them.

LORE: All of them.

SAOIRSE: Then half drowning on the swim back.

LORE: Totally worth it.

SAOIRSE: Definitely worth it. (*raises her cup*) To traveling all over the world from these steps. Greece, Florida...

LORE: The Mediterranean in general.

SAOIRSE: Right. No one else I'd rather spend my days traveling with. Even if it's only us playing pretend.

LORE: (*softly*) God, I'm going to miss you.

SAOIRSE: I'm very missable.

LORE: You are. Maybe we'll see each other again, in the future.

SAOIRSE: Sweet Lore, you're the scientist, you know that won't happen.

LORE: Stranger things have happened.

SAOIRSE: (*not convinced*) Okay. Maybe.

LORE: So you stay strong. You stay sane and healthy and hopeful and strong.

SAOIRSE: You too.

LORE: I'll give it a go.

SAOIRSE: I'm going to miss you too, you know. So much.

LORE: I know. But hey, pass the bottle back. We still have time.

SAOIRSE: The sun?

LORE: She's setting a little slower.

SAOIRSE: Very kind of her.

LORE: (*holding up her cup*) To the sun. To everything she's given us. Food and warmth and a little extra time.

SAOIRSE: Hear, hear! (*grabbing the bottle*) To the earth!

LORE: To the earth!

SAOIRSE: And the days we have left.

LORE: Dark.

SAOIRSE: Very. But I'm tipsy. Dark tipsy.

LORE: Not sparkly?

SAOIRSE: Nope. Or if so, dark sparkles, like Formica.

> (*Beat of quiet.*)

LORE: Saoirse. What I would give...

SAOIRSE: For what?

LORE: To be sitting at a coffee shop with you, again.

SAOIRSE: The outline of that freaking bright shade of lipstick you used to wear on the side of the cup?

LORE: Yeah. Talking about nothing but talking about

nothing for hours.

SAOIRSE: People watching. Because people were outside. Because it wasn't too hot.

LORE: What I would give for you not to go to California.

SAOIRSE: I know. It's been wonderful. All of it. No matter what it's like out there, this, you and me and growing up here? It's only been good.

LORE: You and me and the ocean.

SAOIRSE: Hmm.

(*SAOIRSE looks up at the sky, checking the time by looking at the sun.*)

SAOIRSE: Time to go.

LORE: No.

SAOIRSE: Yes.

LORE: A few more minutes. A few more moments.

SAOIRSE: A breath. A beat. I have to go.

LORE: There's this photo I found. You're beaming at the camera, the sun behind you, and yet your smile outshines the sun. You look like you're the happiest person in the world.

SAOIRSE: You took the photo?

LORE: Yes.

SAOIRSE: Then I probably was.

> (*They look at each other, SAOIRSE makes a move to stand up*.
>
> *Blackout.*)

Leaving the Universe

by Barbara Bryan

CAST OF CHARACTERS:

Hector
Male Customer #1
Male Customer #2
Female Customer #1
Female Customer #2

SETTING:

A small folding table with a cash box surrounded by stacks of cardboard boxes. Cardboard signs printed with black marker:
YARD SALE —>
EVERYTHING GOES
<— YARD SALE
DEALS

TIME:

The Present

ADDITIONAL NOTES:

Production History:
- Run of the Mill Theatre (Baltimore, MD)
  - Variations on Fear Festival
- New Jersey Repertory Theatre (Long Branch, NJ)
  - Theatre Brut Festival
- Black Dog (Snoqualmie, WA)
  - Black Dog Theater Festival

SCENE: MALE CUSTOMER enters, wanders around, surveys the boxes. HECTOR enters, wiping his brow, stands near the cash box and observes MALE CUSTOMER.

MALE CUSTOMER #1:   Packing it all up and moving, eh? Where you heading?

HECTOR: Some place better than this.

MALE CUSTOMER #1:   Maybe you just need a fresh start. You know what they say...Better days ahead. Go west, young man...Get your kicks on Route 66...

HECTOR: Go West? I was thinking it was either gonna be north or south.

MALE CUSTOMER #1:   You don't want to go north, take my word. It gets pretty damn cold up there. For my money, I'd head south. You got hot days and sizzling nights... That's where I'd go, if I wasn't going west. (*peering inside a couple of boxes*) Say, there's nothing in these boxes.

HECTOR: One man's trash is another man's treasure.

MALE CUSTOMER #1: What're you talking about? These boxes are empty.

HECTOR: Everybody's got different taste—

MALE CUSTOMER #1: Taste? The sign says "Deals". You got nothing here.

HECTOR: What kind of deal are you looking for?

MALE CUSTOMER #1: I'll know it when I see it.

HECTOR: Maybe you just haven't looked hard enough. (*beat*) What? You stopped by thinking you're gonna walk away with high quality stuff for pennies on the dollar? Am I right?

MALE CUSTOMER #1: Not pennies—

HECTOR: Guys like you kill me.

(*FEMALE CUSTOMER #1 ENTERS. She looks inside the boxes.*)

FEMALE CUSTOMER #1: Wow! This is great stuff!

HECTOR: Everything's original. I don't sell knock-offs.

FEMALE CUSTOMER #1: You never see originals anymore.

MALE CUSTOMER #1: That box is empty.

FEMALE CUSTOMER #1:   What is he? Blind?

HECTOR: He just doesn't recognize the real thing.

FEMALE CUSTOMER #1:   (*lifting a box*) How much is this?

HECTOR: Fifty bucks for the box.

FEMALE CUSTOMER #1:   Cool. I'll take it. (*pulls fifty dollars out of her purse and gives it to him*)

HECTOR: You got yourself a deal there.

FEMALE CUSTOMER #1:   Thank you.

(*She departs.*

MALE CUSTOMER #1 peers inside another box, then lifts it up.)

HECTOR: Hey! Be careful with that.

MALE CUSTOMER #1:   What's this supposed to be?

HECTOR: It's not supposed to be anything. It is what it is.

MALE CUSTOMER #1:   Well, what is it?

HECTOR: Quit jerking me around. (*beat*) Do you have a kid?

MALE CUSTOMER #1:   Yeah.

HECTOR: He'd know what it is.

MALE CUSTOMER #1:   How do you know?

HECTOR: Any kid would know what this
is. If you walked in the house with one of these, your kid would
be screaming his head off. You'd be a hero.

MALE CUSTOMER #1:   Okay. I'll give you five bucks for
it.

HECTOR: Are you crazy?

MALE CUSTOMER #1:   Alright, six.

HECTOR: You're a pain in the ass, you
know that? You think you can be a hero for six dollars? What
do you think this is—1970?

MALE CUSTOMER #1:   How much do you want?

HECTOR: I'm not even going to sell it to
you. The blue light special's over...done...finito.

   (*FEMALE CUSTOMER #1 returns.*)

FEMALE CUSTOMER #1:   Do you have any more of those?

HECTOR: It's your lucky day, lady.

   (*He pushes MALE CUSTOMER #1's box toward her.*)

FEMALE CUSTOMER #1:   (*looking inside the box*) Oh...my...
god!

MALE CUSTOMER #1:   Hey, that one's mine.

HECTOR: And since you're a repeat customer, I'll give you a real deal on the second one.

FEMALE CUSTOMER #1:   Are you kidding?

MALE CUSTOMER #1:   (*pulling out his wallet*) Here's twenty.

HECTOR: (*ignoring him*) Forty bucks.

FEMALE CUSTOMER #1:   I can't believe this. You're practically giving it away. (*pulls forty dollars from her purse and gives it to Hector*) What else have you got here? I was so excited, I forgot to look in the other boxes.

HECTOR: It doesn't cost anything to look.

FEMALE CUSTOMER #1:   (*looks in another box*) This one's empty.

      (*She pushes it aside – MALE CUSTOMER grabs it.*)

MALE CUSTOMER #1:   I'll take it.

      (*She opens another box. HECTOR glances inside.*)

HECTOR: They're not making any more like this. Once they're gone, that's it.

FEMALE CUSTOMER #1:   Where on earth did you find them? I've been searching high and low...

MALE CUSTOMER #1:   Let me have a look.

FEMALE CUSTOMER #1:   (*blocks him*) I saw them first.

HECTOR: You bundle up with a couple of these babies and you're gonna notice a big difference in your gravity bill.

FEMALE CUSTOMER #1:   My bill's triple what it was last year. (*beat*) Jeez, remember when gravity was free?

HECTOR: Dream on, sister. You'll never see those days again.

MALE CUSTOMER #1:   Who's charging for gravity?

FEMALE CUSTOMER #1:   What planet is he living on? I'll take the whole box.

HECTOR: They're not cheap—but they'll pay for themselves in a month.

FEMALE CUSTOMER #1:   How much?

HECTOR: Since you're a repeat customer, I'll let you have them for one-seventy.

FEMALE CUSTOMER #1:   (*paying him*) Thank you. You're a godsend.

HECTOR: Need some help carrying them?

FEMALE CUSTOMER #1:   No, I've got them. You have another customer here.

HECTOR: Who? Him? He's not buying anything.

MALE CUSTOMER #1:   I'm buying this.

FEMALE CUSTOMER #1: That one's empty, Mister. (*to Hector*) Maybe he picked up the wrong box.

HECTOR: What do you want an empty box for? Just take it.

MALE CUSTOMER #1:   (*taking out his wallet*) I'll pay you. How much is it.

HECTOR: Don't insult me.

FEMALE CUSTOMER #1: Maybe he's moving. Are you moving?

MALE CUSTOMER #1:   No. I was just driving around. (*nodding toward Hector*) He's the one who's moving. He's leaving the universe.

FEMALE CUSTOMER #1: Cool. How long are you gonna be gone?

HECTOR: That remains to be seen.

FEMALE CUSTOMER #1: (*to Male Customer*) If you need any boxes after I put my stuff in the trunk...

MALE CUSTOMER #1:   I'm not moving.

HECTOR: I'm getting ready to close up soon. You're gonna have to move. (*to Female Customer*) He's heading west, driving out Route 66...trying to get some kicks. Isn't that right, Chief?

FEMALE CUSTOMER #1: Oh, they closed Route 66. Didn't you hear?

MALE CUSTOMER #1: What! Who closed it?

FEMALE CUSTOMER #1: The highway closers.

HECTOR: I heard that, too. Somebody was threatening to blow it up.

MALE CUSTOMER #1: Blow up Route 66? For cryin' out loud, what's going on? They can't close Route 66. How's anybody going to go west?

FEMALE CUSTOMER #1: You can't go west anymore.

HECTOR: Just north or south.

MALE CUSTOMER #1: (*in a daze, carrying his box*) Can't go west? How am I going to get home?

FEMALE CUSTOMER #1: (*departing with her box, calling after him*) You can't go home either. (*whistling a few bars of "Get Your Kicks on Route 66"*) But I'll show you where you can get some kicks.

MALE CUSTOMER #1: Huh?

FEMALE CUSTOMER #1: If you can't go home, you'll need a room...somewhere.

(*MALE CUSTOMER #1 follows her.*)

HECTOR: (*calling out after them*) Watch out for black ice. If you don't see it, it'll kill you.

(HECTOR *pulls a batch of flattened cardboard boxes from under the table and begins assembling, then stacking, them.*

FEMALE CUSTOMER #2 enters, looks around.)

FEMALE CUSTOMER #2:   This isn't really a yard. It's more like an intersection. A corner.

HECTOR: So what's the problem?

FEMALE CUSTOMER #2:   A yard sale is supposed to be in a yard.

HECTOR: You're complaining about the location?

FEMALE CUSTOMER #2:   It's not a complaint, just an observation. What are you selling?

HECTOR: It's all right here, lady. Look to your heart's content.

FEMALE CUSTOMER #2:   (*looks in a few boxes*) There's not much left.

HECTOR: There's still plenty of good deals here. (*pushing a box toward her*) This, for instance.

FEMALE CUSTOMER #2:   (*looking inside the box*) Oh, I don't care for that color.

HECTOR: If you don't like the color, just dye it.

FEMALE CUSTOMER 2:   But who uses these anymore? I mean—

HECTOR: Half the people in the world would give their eye teeth for one of these. And you're bitchin' about the color.

FEMALE CUSTOMER #2:   Turquoise went out in the—

HECTOR: That's not turquoise, it's teal. Teal's gonna be hot this fall. (*grabs the box*) But if you don't want it...

FEMALE CUSTOMER #2:   (*looking in another box*) Oh, now here's something... (*reaches in and pulls out something very tiny, almost invisible, from the corner of the box*)

HECTOR: Let me see that.

> (*FEMALE CUSTOMER #2: opens her palm for an instant, then closes it quickly.*)

HECTOR: How'd that get in there? That's not for sale.

FEMALE CUSTOMER #2:   The sign says "Everything Goes". It's got to be for sale.

HECTOR: Well it's not.

FEMALE CUSTOMER #2:   Why not?

HECTOR: Personal reasons.

FEMALE CUSTOMER #2:   Oh, come on now. How could this possibly have sentimental value? (*beat*) Besides, you're leaving the universe, you can't take it with you.

HECTOR: I'll carry it in my pocket. I might need it. (*Hector lunges for it*) Gimme that!

> (*He knocks it out of her hand. It rolls away, down into a storm drain.*)

HECTOR: (*continuing*) Now look what you did. You better leave, right now.

FEMALE CUSTOMER #2:   I'm not finished looking.

HECTOR: You weren't invited to this event. Where's your invitation?

FEMALE CUSTOMER #2:   To a yard sale?

HECTOR: That's right. I've got the list right here. (*scanning a sheet of scrap paper*) I don't see your name on it.

FEMALE CUSTOMER #2:   You don't even know my name.

HECTOR: I don't know your face either. This is a special sale—for repeat customers only.

> (*MALE CUSTOMER #2 enters.*)

HECTOR: (*continuing*) Here's one now. How was your trip, sir?

MALE CUSTOMER #2:   My trip? Oh, it was fine.

HECTOR: How's the family?

MALE CUSTOMER #2:   They're fine. Thanks for asking.

HECTOR: Have a look around. There's still plenty of deals.

MALE CUSTOMER #2:   Looks like I got here just in time. (*picks up a box*) How much do you want for this?

HECTOR: As a matter of fact, I set that one aside especially for you. It's ten dollars.

MALE CUSTOMER #2:   Thank you. I'll take it.

        (*He pays and departs.*)

FEMALE CUSTOMER #2:   So how did he get an invitation?

HECTOR: He didn't do it by coming in here and destroying the merchandise.

FEMALE CUSTOMER #2:   That was an accident. I'm sorry. (*beat*) How often do you hold these sales?

HECTOR: On major holidays: Groundhog's Day – if he doesn't see his shadow. Great American Smokeout Day. And "Return Shopping Carts to the Supermarket Day".

FEMALE CUSTOMER #2:   So people just show up and buy boxes?

HECTOR: They buy what is in the boxes.

FEMALE CUSTOMER #2:   So, if I bought something at this sale, I'd get invited to your next one?

HECTOR: No.

FEMALE CUSTOMER #2:   Why not?

HECTOR: The special sales are for repeat customers. If you bought something, you'd just be a customer. Not a repeat customer.

FEMALE CUSTOMER #2:   How could I ever get to be a repeat customer?

HECTOR: Hell if I know.

FEMALE CUSTOMER #2:   That's not fair.

HECTOR: Who ever told you life's fair? Life is not fair.

FEMALE CUSTOMER #2:   This is a hustle, right?

HECTOR: (*still simmering over the loss of his small object*) No.

(*He packs up the remaining boxes and deposits them in front of FEMALE CUSTOMER #2.*)

FEMALE CUSTOMER #2:   (*musing*) This can't be legit... (*suddenly realizing that Hector is leaving the boxes, the cash box, the business*) Hey! Where are you going? I don't want all this....What am I supposed to do with this?

HECTOR: (*calling back as he exits*) Watch out for black ice. If you don't see it, it'll kill you.

END

A SCENE FROM
*Mary Doesn't Wear
Red Lipstick*

by Cameron Sheppard

CAST OF CHARACTERS:

Mama
Deacon Kincaid
Francis Kincaid, daughter of Deacon Kincaid, a
compassionate young woman struggling
to understand her sexuality in the light
of the Catholic Church.
Sarah Grace, 17, female, an ambitious and clever
aspiring journalist. Francis' classmate.
Angela, 16, female, Francis' best childhood friend
and first love.

SETTING:

Contemporary American household, Francis Kincaid's
bedroom

TIME:

10 o'clock on a Friday night

ADDITIONAL NOTES:

When performing this scene as a short play, the opening bit of
dialogue between Francis and the characters of Mama and
Deacon Kincaid may be omitted, and the performance may
begin with Francis entering her bedroom.

The Kincaid household. MAMA and DEACON KINCAID are sitting downstairs, watching television.

FRANCIS: Okay, I know I'm late, but I promise / it was important.

MAMA: It's almost ten! What are you doing / at school until ten o'clock?

DEACON KINCAID: Were you vaping in the parking lot? You know we just suspended Josephine -

FRANCIS: I was helping Maggie with her locker!

DEACON KINCAID: Oh.

FRANCIS: I'm sorry.

MAMA: Honey, don't be sorry. You were being a good friend.

FRANCIS: Right...Did Sarah Grace —

MAMA: Oh, I let her up in your room.

FRANCIS: You what?!

(*FRANCIS runs to her room and throws open the door.*

Lights up on FRANCIS KINCAID's bedroom. A crucifix hangs above FRANCIS' twin bed. A small collage of pictures and quotes adorns the wall above her desk, the only deviation from the austere simplicity of the room.

SARAH GRACE sits on FRANCIS' bed. She's found FRANCIS' contraband Playboy and is flipping through it. FRANCIS bursts into the room, returning late from rehearsal. SARAH GRACE holds the magazine a little higher.)

SARAH GRACE: (*casually*) Hey, Fran.

FRANCIS: (*pure panic*) That's not mine.

SARAH GRACE: No?

FRANCIS: It's...my cousin's.

SARAH GRACE: You know this is all online now, right?

FRANCIS: He's - Amish.

SARAH GRACE: (*playing along*) Hmm...and your cousin is
staying with you?

FRANCIS: For the, uh, Rums - Rumspr -

SARAH GRACE: Rumspringa?

FRANCIS: Yes, yeah - Wanted to see if he liked electricity - hated it. So he left really early this morning to go back to the...colony.

SARAH GRACE: Convenient.

FRANCIS: He was only here for a few days. And he's kind of weird, honestly—

SARAH GRACE   (*breaks, laughing*) As much as I love watching this, you don't have to make up a story about—

FRANCIS: I'm not!

SARAH GRACE: (*smiles*) You are the worst liar I've ever met. But you've got a good eye for vintage lesbian literature.

FRANCIS: I'm not - that's not - I'm not lesbian.

SARAH GRACE: Oh, sorry. Bi?

FRANCIS: No! I'm not anything.

SARAH GRACE: It's not something you can be into, Fran. You are or you aren't.

FRANCIS: (*grabs magazine from Sarah Grace*) Well, I'm not... Save your support for people who actually need it...Why were you looking around my room anyways?

SARAH GRACE: (*a little too innocently*) I wasn't. It was on the floor.

FRANCIS: Oh. I could've sworn I put - he put it away.

SARAH GRACE: Well, maybe he didn't see it... You know, since he can't turn on the light.

(*FRANCIS tries to suppress a grin.*)

SARAH GRACE: (*continuing*) Snickerdoodle?

FRANCIS   (*sitting on her bed*) Sure, thanks.

(*SARAH GRACE pulls out a high tech field recorder.*)

SARAH GRACE: Ready to trash Father Wesley?

FRANCIS: Woah. That's a super nice, um—

SARAH GRACE: Field recorder.

FRANCIS: Right.

SARAH GRACE: Worked all summer for it.

FRANCIS: That expensive?

SARAH GRACE: It's got four mic inputs, compression, automatic gain control, a 128 gig capacity, thirty hours of battery life, and it'll pick up sounds twenty-five meters away. It's an investment.

FRANCIS: I understood, like, half of that. But it looks legit.

SARAH GRACE: I told you I'm serious about this... I know it's just a stupid high school paper and no one really reads it anyways, but when you put your name on something...

FRANCIS: You want it to be good.

SARAH GRACE: Yeah, but I...we got the forms to order caps and gowns yesterday and I started thinking about everything, I guess. I've spent so much time on this fucking paper, I don't really...I'm not even friends with anyone.

FRANCIS: We're friends.

SARAH GRACE: Well, yeah, but we could've been friends two years ago. And now...I know this sounds stupid, but no one's gonna even remember I was there.

FRANCIS: I will.

SARAH GRACE: No, I mean—

FRANCIS: You made something that's gonna keep going. You changed it and you - and you cared even when nobody did.

> (*SARAH GRACE grabs FRANCIS in a bear hug. FRANCIS hesitates at first, but eventually melts into it before they both pull away.*)

SARAH GRACE: Sorry, I didn't mean to rant -

FRANCIS: You're fine.

SARAH GRACE: Alright, uh, any ideas for the culture section?

> (*LIGHTS DOWN.*

Gregorian chants play while SARAH GRACE moves to sleep on FRANCIS' bed.

FRANCIS sits on the floor, typing.)

FRANCIS: "This year, the theatre department had planned to produce Into the Woods."

(SARAH GRACE snores softly. FRANCIS turns to glance at her and then turns back to refocus on her laptop.)

FRANCIS: *(continuing)* "However, the new administration has requested that the department produce a more faith-based show. With a forty-year-old man as the lead, of course, because God forbid a girl could play Jesus—"

(SARAH GRACE snores again.

FRANCIS turns and looks a bit longer this time. She turns her head back to the paper and rubs her eyes.)

FRANCIS: *(continuing)* Hail Mary, full of grace, the Lord is with thee. Blessed art thou amongst women and blessed is the fruit of thy womb—

(ANGELA enters from behind, unnoticed. She is a figment of FRANCIS' imagination.)

ANGELA: Still doing that, huh?

FRANCIS: Not a good time, Angela.

ANGELA: Is it ever?

(*She crosses to FRANCIS.*)

ANGELA: (*continuing*) You never told me why you do - that.

FRANCIS: You know why.

ANGELA: (*in her best priestly voice*) A "Hail Mary" a day keeps the homosexuality away.

(*FRANCIS returns to her laptop in search of a distraction.*)

ANGELA: (*continuing*) Who told you to?

FRANCIS   (*beat*) Father Ed.

ANGELA: (*glancing at Sarah Grace*) Looks like it's working.

FRANCIS: Shut up.

ANGELA: Oh, c'mon, I'm not gonna tell... She looks pretty cute when she's sleeping.

FRANCIS: She looks like a normal sleeping person.

(*ANGELA crosses to sit next to SARAH GRACE on the bed.*)

ANGELA: Don't you ever get tired of it?

(*FRANCIS looks longingly at SARAH GRACE.*)

ANGELA: (*continuing*) Fran, what's worse - lying to other people or lying to yourself? Cuz' you're doing both.

FRANCIS: Would you just - you make it sound like I'm a criminal or something! I didn't do anything / wrong.

ANGELA: I'm not accusing you of - Jesus, if you'd just say it, Fran—

FRANCIS: I'm not - I'm not gonna confess to something that I—

ANGELA: Well, good, because I don't know any priest who'd be awake at three in the morning.

FRANCIS: Please, just, please leave me alone.

> (*ANGELA moves to sit next to FRANCIS, who is starting to get emotional.*)

ANGELA: You can talk to me.

FRANCIS: I...I can't look at you.

> (*ANGELA studies FRANCIS before taking two chairs from FRANCIS' room. She faces one chair towards the audience and another in the opposite direction.*
>
> *ANGELA puts on a stole and gestures for FRANCIS to sit in the forward-facing chair.*
>
> *She obeys.*)

FRANCIS: (*continuing*) I don't know, Angela. I don't even know how to begin to—

ANGELA: (*donning a priestly voice again*) Forgive me Father for I have...

FRANCIS: (*with a sigh*) Forgive me Father for I have sinned. It has been...well, this is my first fake confession.

ANGELA: A first-timer!

FRANCIS: Yeah. Yeah, I guess.

ANGELA: Mhmm. Go on.

FRANCIS: During this time, I...I started to have feelings for someone, I think. I guess I've always kind of liked them, but now I know them and I can't stop thinking that maybe...maybe they like me too.

ANGELA: And what is it you like about this person?

> (*During FRANCIS' confession, ANGELA leaves, unnoticed.*)

FRANCIS: Well, they—she...she's beautiful. I don't know if she really thinks that about herself, but she is...And her hair is so...soft. When she stands in the light, it looks like a halo. That makes me sound superficial, Father, but it's—it's not just that. It's the look she gets in her eyes when she cares about something. Like, really, really cares about it... Or when she has something funny to tell me, but she can't say it without laughing. And Father, she makes me smile. And I wanna kiss her. And go to the movies with her. And sit and read books together in a cafe. I wanna dress up and take her to fancy restaurants that I definitely can't afford... I want to... I want to love her. (*beat*) So, what's my penance?

SARAH GRACE: (*waking up with a yawn*) Francis? Oh my God, what time is it?

FRANCIS: (*struggling*) Uh, three-thirty, I think.

SARAH GRACE: What are you doing?

FRANCIS: I got, um, tired of sitting on the ground.

SARAH GRACE: Come sit here. Sorry, I didn't mean to crash. Let me finish up the rest.

(*FRANCIS hesitates and then brings the laptop to the bed.*)

FRANCIS: I - I started the fashion section, but you probably should do that. Not really my thing.

SARAH GRACE: Well, the layout's great. Ooh, a "Who Wore It Best." Nice.

FRANCIS: Oh, yeah, um, I thought we could put a box somewhere and have people vote... to get them more interested, maybe.

SARAH GRACE: That's brilliant, Francis.

FRANCIS: (*smiling awkwardly*) It's not, like, anything revolutionary. Just an idea.

SARAH GRACE: We could even do it every week and it doesn't have to be fashion stuff all the time. We can survey about-about, like, real, important issues - not that fashion's not—

FRANCIS: (*can't spit it out fast enough*) Your eyelashes are really long.

SARAH GRACE: What?

FRANCIS: Uh - they're just - yeah.

SARAH GRACE: Francis...

FRANCIS: I'm sorry if that was - if that was weird.
I think I should probably get some sleep, so...

> (*FRANCIS turns away and lays down in her makeshift bed
> on the ground. She begins to pray, falling into her coping
> mechanism. Her prayer is almost a whisper.*)

FRANCIS: (*continuing*) Hail Mary, full of grace, the
Lord is with thee. Blessed art thou amongst women and blessed
is the fruit of thy womb, Jesus. Holy Mary, Mother of God,
Pray for us sinners now and at the hour of our death.

> (*SARAH GRACE sits next to FRANCIS and pulls on
> her blanket. Her actions are careful and deliberate.*)

FRANCIS: (*continuing*) Hail Mary—

SARAH GRACE: Full of grace...

> (*She brushes FRANCIS' hair back and kisses her cheek.*)

SARAH GRACE: (*continuing*) The Lord is with thee.

> (*She unbuttons FRANCIS' shirt.*)

SARAH GRACE: Blessed art thou...

> (*She kisses FRANCIS' lips and then her neck and shoulder.*)

SARAH GRACE: Amongst women...

(She puts her hand on FRANCIS' thigh, looking up for permission, which FRANCIS grants.)

SARAH GRACE: And blessed is the fruit...

(She traces her fingers along FRANCIS' thigh until they disappear under her skirt.)

SARAH GRACE: Of thy womb...

(FRANCIS turns her head. They have almost become Michelangelo's Pietà.)

FRANCIS: Jesus.

END ACT ONE.

To Fix A Dinosaur

by Emma S. Rund

CAST OF CHARACTERS:

Felix, a new resident in the pediatric surgery wing,
recently overwhelmed with the unexpected
weight of life, 29, male
Liz, a mother trying her best to cope while her son
undergoes surgery upstairs, 38, female

SETTING:

The back stairwell of a hospital.

TIME:

The present.

ADDITIONAL NOTES:

Production History:
- Reading at Playpenn (July '19)
  - Directed by Dan O'Neil
- Reading at Chicago Dramatists (November '19)
  - Directed by Devon Hayakawa
- The Hive Collaborative (July '20)
  - Adapted for The Hive Collaborative Short
    Film Festival
- Ensemble Theatre of Chattanooga (September '20)
  - Lights Up! Podcast, Episode 3

SCENE: FELIX, wearing a rumpled T-shirt and jeans and looking completely exhausted, bursts through the second floor doorway and runs down the stairs, escaping from something.

LIZ, wearing the same thing she's had on for two days, bursts through the first floor doorway and into the stairwell carrying a toy dinosaur constructed from Legos.

She is also escaping from something.

LIZ and FELIX collide, and the dinosaur crashes to the floor, breaking into a mess of pieces.

LIZ: FUCK.

FELIX: I am so sorry. I am so so sorry. Are you okay?

                (FELIX tries to touch her arm. She yanks it away out of reflex.)

LIZ: *(snapping)* I'm FINE!

                (FELIX takes a step back, putting his hands up in surrender.)

LIZ: Sorry, it's not you. It's—Well, you know.

FELIX: I'm so sorry about the...what was it?

LIZ: A dinosaur. For my son.

FELIX: Oh, is he...?

            (*FELIX gestures upstairs.*

            LIZ nods.)

LIZ: I couldn't take the waiting anymore, you know? My husband is so fucking calm about it all, and I can't take all that stillness right now, you know? I thought maybe I could get outside this way.

FELIX: (*pointing in the direction he was heading*) The exit's that way. I was just leaving actually. I had to get out of here. If you want to come with me I'll show you.

LIZ: (*shaking her head*) I can't go back in there.

FELIX: I'll just...

            (*He motions to the dinosaur remains and kneels down. He gathers the Legos into a pile and embarks on an attempt to reassemble.*)

LIZ: You don't have to—

FELIX: No, no it was my fault.

LIZ: I really don't know how you're going to do that without the directions.

FELIX: It's a kids toy. It can't be that complicated, right?

LIZ: You'd be surprised. That thing is like rocket science or something. It took me basically all of the last three days to do it.

FELIX: God, I'm sorry.

LIZ: It's okay. I haven't been able to sleep anyways. You know what that's like.

FELIX: Yeah. I don't think anyone sleeps in this place.

LIZ: Yeah. Every time you close your eyes you see your child in pain, so instead you find stupid tasks to distract yourself like building Lego dinosaurs, you know?

(*He turns his focus back to the Legos.*

They're both quiet for a moment.)

LIZ: What's yours in for?

(*FELIX says nothing, but keeps assembling the Legos.*)

LIZ: (*continuing*) You don't have to talk about it. I get it. I still haven't figured out if talking about it makes it better or worse. You'd think after four or five of these I'd have this down to some kind of science, but it seems to get scarier every time. Like, the more surgeries go right, the higher the chances become that the next one will go wrong.

(*FELIX says nothing, just keeps assembling Legos.*)

LIZ: Sometimes I think that if I articulate all the terrible things that could happen, the chances of them actually happening get lower and lower. If I say 'what if my son loses a limb' then he can't actually lose a limb because then the universe would have heard what I said or something, and that's impossible. I thought that. But then yesterday a little girl down the hall had to get her leg amputated. Osteosarcoma. Same as my son. And for a split second I actually thought it was my fault. I thought I spoke it into existence. Of course, that's ridiculous, but...

> (*FELIX says nothing, just keeps assembling Legos. A structure begins to emerge that vaguely resembles a dinosaur if you're really squinting to see it.*
>
> *Finally:*)

FELIX: (*re the Legos*) God I'm so tired I can't see straight. This is impossible.

LIZ: Told you.

FELIX: I really feel awful. I should have been watching where I was going.

LIZ: I'm the one who burst through the door. That's like the number one rule of opening doors: do it slowly.

FELIX: Is it?

LIZ: In case someone like yourself is on the other side.

FELIX: Sure, I guess, but I was so focused on getting out I wasn't even—

LIZ: Besides. It's just a toy. There are more important things.

FELIX: Right. Of course, you're right.

(*But FELIX continues to assemble the Legos.*)

LIZ: You really don't have to do that. You can get back to your... son? daughter?

FELIX: That's okay.

LIZ: Please. I don't want to keep you.

FELIX: You're not keeping me / from anything.

LIZ: Look, we all need to escape sometimes, but—

FELIX: I'll just finish this up / real quick.

LIZ: Please, don't bother—

FELIX: It'll just take / a second.

LIZ: It really doesn't matter.

(*LIZ reaches out for the dinosaur. FELIX pulls it away.*)

FELIX: It does matter. You made it for him.

LIZ: He doesn't even like dinosaurs! I just needed something to do!

FELIX: And I ruined it!

LIZ: I   don't   care   about   the   FUCKING DINOSAUR!

FELIX: I NEED TO FIX IT! I need to fix SOMETHING! I need to fix it. I need to... I need to... I can't...

(*He trails off.*)

LIZ: (*gently*) Forget about the dinosaur.

(*FELIX breaks down.*)

LIZ: It's okay.

(*She slides over next to him and puts an arm around him.*

He says nothing. She picks up the dinosaur.)

LIZ: Kind of a stupid looking thing, isn't it? Doesn't even look like a dinosaur anymore.

FELIX: I messed up.

LIZ: It's okay.

FELIX: No, it really isn't. I really fucked up.

LIZ: We're not talking about the dinosaur anymore, are we?

(*FELIX shakes his head.*)

LIZ: (*continuing*) So you messed up?

(*FELIX nods.*)

LIZ: So what? You're human.

FELIX: This isn't that kind of mistake.

LIZ: What kind of mistake isn't human?

FELIX: A big one.

LIZ: We've all made some big mistakes. You just have to do your best to make it better.

FELIX: I can't.

LIZ: Why not?

FELIX: It's irreparable, what I did.

LIZ: Did you do it on purpose?

FELIX: No! No. God no.

LIZ: Then it doesn't—

FELIX: I didn't mean to—I was just so SO tired, I hadn't really slept in 48 hours, and I'd never done it before, and she said I was ready, that I would be fine, and I thought, I thought if I could just do this perfectly than I could prove myself, and I just... I... I slipped— I don't know. I don't know what happened. I don't—

LIZ: What's your name?

FELIX: Felix.

LIZ: Felix, listen to me. I don't know what you did or why you're so bent out of shape about it, but no honest mistake is completely irreparable.

FELIX: I can't fix this. It's all my fault, and I can't fix it.

(*A long silence.*)

LIZ: Last night I was working on the dinosaur in my son's hospital room. He was sound asleep, completely still, almost peaceful, and I whispered to that little dinosaur, 'what if he dies?' And I thought, 'now he can't possibly because I voiced it. I put the words out into the air, so now it can't happen.' And then I thought of the little girl down the hall. Now I can't stop thinking about all the other children in this place. If a single one of them dies today it's going to be my fault, because I put those words out into the air.

FELIX: That's not your fault.

LIZ: I know that, but a part of me can't help feeling like it—

FELIX: But it's not. You can't kill anybody by wishing that your son won't die.

LIZ: Felix, I know. I'm just saying that maybe this thing you think is your fault isn't really—

FELIX: THIS ISN'T LIKE THAT! I was running away, when I bumped into you. I was running away. She was going to make me face them and I just couldn't. GOD! I was just going to leave them without—

(*Beat.*)

LIZ: Think of it this way. If this big mistake, whatever it is, is important to your child, you have to do everything you can to fix it, but if it doesn't affect your child then forget about it. It doesn't matter right now. Nothing but that child matters right now. Like the dinosaur. Alright?

(*A long pause.*)

FELIX: Alright.

(*FELIX stands up.*)

FELIX: (*continuing*) Thank you.

LIZ: No problem.

FELIX: God, I'm so sorry about the dino—

LIZ: Felix. It doesn't matter.

FELIX: I just feel awful.

LIZ: Look. I forgive you, if that helps.

FELIX: Thank you. I think I should probably go try to... [make amends]

LIZ: Good luck.

(*He takes her hands.*)

FELIX: Good luck to you too.

(*They share a moment. He lets her go. He heads up the stairs and disappears through the top door.*

LIZ starts to pick up the pieces of the dinosaur. She takes apart what FELIX attempted to rebuild, and begins to fix it herself. She knows what she's doing.

The top door opens and FELIX re-enters. He is now wearing a pair of scrubs.

LIZ stares but says nothing.

He walks with purpose down the stairs and stops outside the first floor door, shifting his weight from foot to foot.)

FELIX: I can't do it.

(A long silence.)

LIZ: I think you have to.

(He takes a breath, and walks with purpose out the door.

LIZ doesn't move. She just watches the door.

FELIX's voice drifts into the stairwell from the waiting room.)

FELIX (offstage):   Mr. and Mrs. Caldwell?

(LIZ drops the Legos.)

FELIX (offstage):   Mr. Caldwell, is your wife around?

(LIZ sinks to the ground.)

FELIX (offstage):   Excuse me.

(*The door opens. FELIX is back. He slowly steps into the stairwell.*

FELIX looks at LIZ.)

FELIX: Mrs. Caldwell?

(*LIZ looks at FELIX. BLACKOUT.*)

END OF PLAY.

Iago's Deal

by John Joseph Enright

CAST OF CHARACTERS:

Mephistopheles, the devil
Desdemona
Iago
Othello

SETTING:

Gates of Hell

TIME:

1570

ADDITIONAL NOTES:

Desdemona, Othello, and Iago are characters from Shakespeare's play, *Othello, the Moor of Venice*. This play takes place soon after the events of Shakespeare's play, and imagines the reunion of these characters in the afterlife. The character of Mephistopheles is adopted from Goethe's *Faust*.

SCENE: MEPHISTOPHELES on stage. Enter DESDEMONA, from heaven.

MEPHISTOPHELES:
You grace us with your presence, without warning.

DESDEMONA:
I hear Iago's being hanged this morning.

MEPHISTOPHELES:
Then I expect he should drop in here shortly.

DESDEMONA:
Prince of Lies, your manner's always courtly.
I've never understood why this is so.

MEPHISTOPHELES:
You mean, because I love to visit woe
On unsuspecting souls? But that's just it.
To keep them unsuspecting, I must split
My manner from my matter. That works nicely.
Our guest arrives.

(*Enter IAGO.*)

IAGO:

              Hey! What the hell?

MEPHISTOPHELES:

                      Precisely.
You're at the gates. I think you know my friend.
In fact, I think you caused her bitter end.

IAGO:
Of course. Dear Desdemona. How's Othello?

MEPHISTOPHELES:
He's some floors down. On fire. Lovely fellow.
His jealousy consumes him as we speak.

IAGO:
His passions ran too strong. His mind was weak.
You never should have granted him your hand.

DESDEMONA:
It's true our marriage did not go as planned.
And if I could rewind the hands of life,
I'd much prefer to skip the storm and strife
And marry someone else. I had my share
Of suitors in my day.

IAGO:

              It isn't fair.

DESDEMONA:

                   What's that?

IAGO:
He soaked up everybody's love.

MEPHISTOPHELES:
In every contest, one must rise above
The others. It's a lesson that I learned
The hard way. You might say that it's been burned
Into my heart.

IAGO:
                    That doesn't make it right.

DESDEMONA:
How odd to hear a creature of the night
Discourse to us on what is truly light.

IAGO:
I have a conscience. It's just not pure white
Like yours.

DESDEMONA:
                    I have my flaws.

IAGO:
                                        Oh yeah? Like what?

DESDEMONA:
I could provide a lengthy checklist, but...

MEPHISTOPHELES:
Your lengthy checklist will prove short on knavery.

DESDEMONA:
I'll give you one. I wish I had more bravery.
If I'd been brave, I never would have lied
About that handkerchief. I tried to hide
The fact I'd lost it. That was my undoing.

IAGO:
And what about succumbing to his wooing?
I'd say that lust was lurking in your heart.

DESDEMONA:
It figures that you'd say that. For my part,
I'd say I was impulsive and unwise.
But, God, he was so dazzling to my eyes.

MEPHISTOPHELES:
Please do not say that name while you are here.
I get a most unpleasant jolt of fear
Whenever he is mentioned too specifically.

IAGO:
I have to say he treated you horrifically.

MEPHISTOPHELES:
I would have done much worse to him. In fact
I would have chained him, with no power to act.
But he left me in charge of my domain.
It's not so bad. I really can't complain.

IAGO:
One always can complain – that's my belief.
Whenever one complaint finds some relief,
I move on quickly to my next big beef.

DESDEMONA:
Which brings me to the reason for my visit.

MEPHISTOPHELES:
You're on a mission? Tell me, please, what is it?

DESDEMONA:
Before you cast this fiend into the fire,
Before I must rejoin the floating choir,
I hope that he can help me understand.

IAGO:
A fiery pit – is that what you've got planned?

MEPHISTOPHELES:
It's standard. But you get an extra tweak.

IAGO:
Well toss me in. I vowed I'd never speak
A single word of explanation more.

DESDEMONA:
You're dead now. Reconsider what you swore.

MEPHISTOPHELES:
You held your tongue while stretched upon the rack,
They broke your bones, and still you would not yack.
I quite admire your iron-hard resolve,
But this may be your last chance to evolve
A tiny bit – a way for you to earn
A better situation as you burn.
Instead of being spitted on a skewer,
I'll merely leave you potted like a stewer.

IAGO:
All right. I guess I'll take one torture fewer.
What do you wish to ask at this late date?

DESDEMONA:
How did your hatred ever grow so great,
So grand that it could serve to motivate

These self-destructive actions that you took?
I think an ounce of fore-thought should have shook
You from the execution of your schemes.
You left too many clues, and all your dreams
Turned into nightmares bursting at the seams.
Your own self-interest really should have made
You hit the brakes.

IAGO:
                                My hand was overplayed,
But what's your point?

DESDEMONA:
                                Just this. You bore a grudge
That started as a teeny-tiny smudge
And grew it to a mountain full of sludge.
Why did you do that? What on earth possessed you?

IAGO:
I had my reasons.

DESDEMONA
                                I don't want to test you
About your reasons. That is not my question.
Your reasons were too small. It's my suggestion
Some other hatred wormed into your soul,
Some other hatred that consumed you whole.

IAGO:
Some other hatred? What's your candidate?

DESDEMONA:
I theorize you're brimming with self-hate.

IAGO:
Some things about myself I do detest.
But in some ways, I'm just about the best.
And so, I'd say, I take a balanced view
Of my own failings, and my glories too.
Some men do fall in love with their self-image,
And fight to keep it high above the scrimmage
Of daily dirt. Their ego is a shrine
To sheer perfection. Well, that isn't mine.

DESDEMONA:
My husband had the pride which you describe.

IAGO:
Such people form a vain and boastful tribe.
They see themselves as noble shining heroes,
As if the rest of us were measly zeroes.

DESDEMONA:
And so, you do not care for them, I take it.

IAGO:
When I see such false pride I long to break it,
To smash it to a million shattered pieces.

DESDEMONA:
Such pride insults you, and thereby releases
A passion to wreak havoc on the bearer.

IAGO:
And in this way, I make the world fairer.
Pride is a form of wealth, and it should be
Distributed on earth more evenly.

MEPHISTOPHELES:
Iago, thank you, for thus explicating
The way that virtue motivates your hating.

DESDEMONA:
I wouldn't call that virtue. Not exactly.

MEPHISTOPHELES:
Enough. He has explained it matter-of-factly.
I've honored your request to interview him.
But now the time has come for me to stew him.

IAGO:
And have I, through my words of explanation,
Escaped the skewer in my new location?

MEPHISTOPHELES:
I'm sad to say, it's true. Your lot's improved.

IAGO:
It pains you that my skewer's been removed.
But what if I could offer you a deal?

MEPHISTOPHELES:
I always love a deal. They make me feel
So clever when they work out for the worst.

IAGO:
Well, here's the deal. I'll go back to the first
Punishment that you had me slotted for,
I'll go back to a rod thrust through my core,
If I can, one more time, confront the Moor.

MEPHISTOPHELES:
Let's just be clear about the deal we're making,

Let's not have any hedging or mistaking.
If I produce this person to your face,
And give you some brief time to state your case,
No matter what new truth comes out of it,
You're back to being roasted on a spit.
Correct?

  IAGO:
      Correct.

MEPHISTOPHELES:
         All right. The deal is done.
Great Moor, arise. Come forth and join the fun.

     (*Enter OTHELLO, from hell.*)

  DESDEMONA:
Dear lord.

  OTHELLO:
      Dear Desdemona.

  MEPHISTOPHELES:
             You two, quiet!
I know that your relationship ran riot,
And I can see where you might want to talk,
But that won't be allowed. Feel free to gawk
At one another. Now, Iago, speak.
Confront Othello. Vent your words of pique.
You paid me for the privilege very well.

  IAGO:
How glad I am to see you here in hell.
Without my intervention, it's a given,
You someday would have ended up in heaven.

OTHELLO:
Your neck looks like it has been somewhat lengthened.

IAGO:
My neck was stretched, but my resolve was strengthened.
I never loved you, Moor, I always hated.

OTHELLO:
You loved me in your way, but you were fated
To kill the ones you loved, including me.
I grasp that now. Unholy jealousy
Turns love to hate. Just look within your heart.

IAGO:
What? No! I hated you right from the start.

OTHELLO:
You think that now, but give it time, you'll see.
We'll be together for eternity,
And we'll have lots of time to sort it out.

IAGO:
Eternity? What is this all about?

MEPHISTOPHELES:
The place you're slotted for, is right beside him.

IAGO:
Until the end of time I can deride him?
But wait a minute, what about our deal?

MEPHISTOPHELES:
A lovely deal. It really was a steal.

IAGO:
I didn't need to trade my skewering for
A final chance to rail against the Moor!

MEPHISTOPHELES:
If only you had thought to broach that topic!
But, no, your hatred made you too myopic.
Off with you now! Both of you! Through the gate!
No more delay. Hell doesn't care to wait.

(*Exit IAGO toward hell.*)

OTHELLO:
Dear wife, I'm sorry.

DESDEMONA:
                    Go. It's far too late.

(*Exit OTHELLO toward hell.*)

MEPHISTOPHELES:
Dear lady, did you find here what you came for?

DESDEMONA:
I do not know. Perhaps there is no name for
Whatever thing is churning in his innards.

MEPHISTOPHELES:
You really ought to take my class on sinners.

DESDEMONA:
I find I've had my fill of lower learning.
Farewell, Dark Prince, I leave you to your burning.

(Exit DESDEMONA towards heaven.)

END OF PLAY.

Chalked

by Alexander Scally

94

CAST OF CHARACTERS:

Leonard, early 50s, black, equally friendly and
caustic
Young Woman, jogging through Leonard's
neighborhood
Will, Leonard's next-door neighbor, mid-20s,
open-race, hipster aesthetic, relaxed vibe
Laura, Jamie's partner, late 20s–30s, white,
thoughtful and optimistic
Jamie, Laura's partner, late 20s–30s, white,
inquisitive and skeptical
Denise, early 30s, black, professional and poised

SETTING:

A neighborhood in West Baltimore.

TIME:

The present.

ADDITIONAL NOTES:

Chalked premiered in Glass Mind Theatre's Brainstorm 5: Ties
That Bind Festival (2015, Baltimore) with the following cast:

Leonard . . . Daniel Carter   Will . . . Rob Vary
Young Woman . . . Dana Woodson   Laura . . . Erin Boots
Jamie . . . Lee Conderacci   Denise . . . Kay-Megan Washington

SCENE: Lights rise on a street in Baltimore to the opening bars of Gil Scott-Heron's "Pieces of a Man." The street is represented by a bare stage, furnished with two sets of porch steps. We see LEONARD sitting on his stoop, lighting his morning cigarette. A YOUNG WOMAN jogs by, stopping to check her heart rate in front of the older man's porch. She looks down and notices a large, obscured line of chalk on the sidewalk. She stares at the line, bewildered, but she moves along.

   WILL enters, mug in hand, and sits on the adjoining stoop and checks in with LEONARD.

WILL: Hey, Leonard. How's it goin'?

LEONARD: Oh, I'm just fine. Knee's acting up, though.

WILL: Think it'll rain?

LEONARD: I'm arthritic, not a damn farmer.

WILL: Can I get a drag?

LEONARD: Give me a sip of that coffee, and we'll call it even.

WILL: *(handing mug to Leonard)* All yours.

LEONARD: (*takes large sip, spits onto ground*) The hell is that?!

WILL: That's high-grade, Jamaican Blue Mountain, my man.

LEONARD: They naming coffee after weed now? (*smells mug*) Tastes like they slipped some in, too. (*hands back mug, imitating Will*) All yours, my man.

WILL: Thanks, Leonard. I gotta hit the road. Getting observed today, so I gotta be extra early.

LEONARD: Go ahead and teach those children, William. They say they're the future, you know.

WILL: (*rubs Leonard's shoulder*) Got it. Have a good one.

LEONARD: You, too.

WILL: (*steps on chalk, wipes off shoe*) Where'd this chalk come from?

LEONARD: Mystery to me.

WILL: Looks like that Hopkins kid that lives above me puked and tried to clear the evidence. Gotta love Thirsty Thursdays. (*looks at watch*) Shit, I'm running late. See ya, Len.

> (*LEONARD puts out his cigarette and remains on stoop. JAMIE and LAURA, a young couple, walk by holding hands and stop next to the stoop.*)

JAMIE: (*to Leonard*) Good morning.

LEONARD: 'Morning.

JAMIE: We're here to look at the second floor apartment. Are you the landlord?

LEONARD: You must be looking for Denise. Lives over in the county, so she's probably stuck in some traffic. Didn't know she was showing it today.

LAURA: We called her yesterday after we saw the 'For Rent' sign and she mentioned she was looking for a tenant right away. What do you think of the neighborhood?

LEONARD: Sure ain't like what it was 40 years ago.

JAMIE: You grew up here?

LEONARD: Yup. Big, blue rowhouse about a half mile from here.

JAMIE: The three-story house on Mosley? (*Leonard nods; to Laura*) We drove past there yesterday, remember?

LAURA: Oh, yeah. It's a shame there are no other houses there.

LEONARD: Yep, South Mosley. Mother, father, four brothers and two sisters.

LAURA: Aw, I wish I had a big family like that. Do they still live around here?

LEONARD: Some of 'em.

JAMIE: It's great to meet someone who's actually from here, for once. Are there a lot of families on the block?

LEONARD: Oh, yeah. Got a lot of folks who been here a long time. They stay inside, mostly, but they're here.

LAURA: Really? It seems like the kind of place where everyone would know each other.

LEONARD: What you mean by that?

LAURA: (*checks in with Jamie*) Nevermind. Is anyone living in the apartment now?

LEONARD: Nah. A fella named Jim lived here up until a few months ago. Used to call him 'Jim Rat'.

LAURA: He worked out a lot?

LEONARD: Something like that. Used to round up a couple rats from the alley once a month and cook 'em up in a stew. Smelled the place up. I suppose that was the man's right, though.

JAMIE: Are you serious?

LEONARD: Maybe.

LAURA: (*noticing she's standing on chalk line*) Oh, I didn't see that before. I used to love playing with sidewalk chalk.

JAMIE: Used to, like... last week?

LAURA: Very funny. (*to Leonard*) I run a daycare center, so I'm no stranger to toddler street art. Looks like it's been here a few days, though. I wonder who drew it.

LEONARD: Mystery to me.

(Long, awkward pause. DENISE enters quickly, breaking the silence.)

DENISE: *(to Jamie & Laura)* Denise Webber, nice to meet you both. So sorry I'm late.

JAMIE: Totally fine. I'm Jamie, and this is Laura.

LAURA: Nice to meet you, Ms. Webber. I'm Laura. We were just talking to… what's your name, sir?

LEONARD: Leonard. Leonard Dobbs.

DENISE: Thank you for keeping them company, Mr. Dobbs. *(directing couple to stairs)* You can go ahead, I'll be up shortly.

        (JAMIE and LAURA exit.)

LEONARD: *(after a moment)* Mr. Dobbs? Like I ain't known you your whole life.

DENISE: The place has been on the market for three months, Leonard. Evan and I are about to take out a second mortgage on the house.

LEONARD: Why don't you move here, you and the boys?

DENISE: Where would they go to school, Central Booking Elementary? No, thank you…

LEONARD: *(cutting her off)* You watch your mouth, young lady! If it wasn't for your Mama and Daddy busting their butts to buy this house, you wouldn't have nothing to keep your lights on now. You need to take pride in that, pride in where you came from.

DENISE: They'd be proud that I've moved on and am raising my sons to be good men. Look around, Leonard. When was the last time you saw a boy around here who wasn't hustlin' or looking over his shoulder? I refuse to let my children be surrounded by foot soldiers and thug recruiters. Think about what your mother's been through, burying two boys before she was even your age. I'll never understand how you can hold onto this place.

LEONARD: So, you bringin' in some white folks to clean up the place?

DENISE: It's not about race, Leonard. These are people who actually see the potential in this neighborhood and don't sit around waiting for the next month's check to arrive.

LEONARD: Hm, sounds like an opportunity. Opportunistic, I'd say.

DENISE: You…. You know what? We'll discuss this some other time. I'm going upstairs.

LEONARD: Go on. Better get 'em to seal the deal before they find out we ain't got yoga studios yet.

DENISE: Leonard, please. (*sees chalk*) …Oh God, did they see this? How long has this been here?

LEONARD: Mystery to me.

DENISE: I need to go upstairs.

(DENISE exits.

A moment of silence. Stage lights narrow to frame the image of a chalk-outlined body behind LEONARD. LEONARD *rises, slowly and with purpose, as the sound of various sirens swell and vanish. He looks at the chalked ground, pauses, and quietly begins to speak.)*

LEONARD:
Step over the chalk line, never stop to hold
Fathers, brothers, sons; bright, strong and bold
Thousands of 'good' men, still bought and sold
Can't get no steady foot to rent or own
Just got Cash for Gold, Bail Bonds for loan
Live in a glass house, ain't got no stones
But a few blocks away, new grass is grown
Puttin' a Starbucks on the cobblestones
Shots fire out, leave a stack of bones
Urban Plight King get a brand new throne.

Boys on the block, don't know they coda
Hand 'em a gun, drugs, cuffs, or diploma
No choice to be made, ain't good enough
Take a strong, black man, grind 'em into dust
Chalk the corpses out, fill the caskets up
Don't know what to do with the rest of us
Layin' on the ground, just let 'em bleed
Who will it be? Mystery to me.

(LEONARD pulls out another cigarette, places it in his mouth, and pulls chalk from his pocket as the final verse of "Pieces of a Man" plays.

He traces the outline of a body on the ground, beginning to fill in details as the lights dim. Blackout.)

Cake Day

by Alexander Scally

Cast of Characters:

Jada, quality assurance specialist
Alonso, assistant
Warren, non-exempt employee
Sheila, office manager
Derek, director of human resources

Setting:

The stage is decorated with chairs and desks to represent a contemporary office.

Time:

Unknown.

SCENE ONE

A spotlight shines on JADA, sitting in a swivel chair. When a character speaks, a light shines to reveal them in swivel chairs.

JADA: Honestly, it seemed like any other day. I swiped in, sat down, and got started with my work. We had a meeting scheduled at 10 a.m., which was typical for a Tuesday.

ALONSO: I really didn't expect it. I've been with the company for three years and think of my co-workers as family. I've always considered this place safe. Until that day.

WARREN: You never think it could happen here. Sure, you've heard about it happening in other places, but it didn't seem possible. You can prepare for these things as best as you can but, ultimately, there's no way to know when it's coming.

SHEILA: I keep picturing the days leading up to it. Was it something that we did? Could have done something differently?

JADA: No.

ALONSO: No.

WARREN: No.

SHEILA: Absolutely not.

JADA: That was the day… that Cake Day was cancelled.

(*Lights fade.*)

Scene Two

Lights rise on the group sitting around a large table.

DEREK: Ok, everyone. Thank you for arriving so promptly. The first item on today's agenda is an update regarding our monthly birthday celebrations, where a cake is brought in for everyone to share. Due to a rise in food allergies and other dietary restrictions, Cake Day will no longer take place.

ALONSO: Are you serious, Derek?

DEREK: Yes, Alonso. If you'll recall, a survey was sent out last week where it was determined, by vote, that the majority of the office feels it's no longer necessary. And you know the polls don't lie.

JADA: You can take that poll and shove it up your ass!

WARREN/SHEILA: Jada!

JADA: I'm sorry, I spoke a bit out of turn. It's

just that, as you all know, it's been a difficult year for my department. We had so many layoffs last quarter that I'm basically doing the job of three people. I also know that Sheila's interns are starting to burn out.

SHEILA: That's true.

JADA: What I'm saying is that we have so little to look forward to. While Red Velvet April was a little stale and last December's ice cream cake was a bust, we need that one day where we can all come together and celebrate.

WARREN: She's got a point. Can't we find some alternative?

DEREK: I wish we could, but our resources are spread thin, Warren, and we have to be sensitive to the needs of all of our employees.

SHEILA: It was Vanessa, wasn't it?

DEREK: What? What was Vanessa?

WARREN: I think you're onto something.

ALONSO: Definitely.

JADA: It has to be. Casein free?

SHEILA: What even IS casein?

WARREN: I used to think it was a type of slow dance.

ALONSO: Me too. Weird!

DEREK: I assure you that this has been a concern addressed by multiple people this year. And the decision is final. Let's move to our next item.

(Lights fade. The group exits.)

SCENE THREE

Lights rise. The chairs have returned to their areas from Scene One. Characters swivel around to address each other. JADA is the first to enter the space. WARREN follows shortly behind. They sit in their respective chairs.

JADA: Good morning!

WARREN: Wadda tu!

JADA: What was that?

WARREN: Skee woop!

        (*SHEILA enters and sits.*)

SHEILA: Good morning, Jada. Warren.

WARREN: (*quietly*) Choo whip.

JADA: (*to Sheila*) What is Warren doing?

SHEILA: Oh, you didn't see the email about him yesterday?

JADA: No.

SHEILA: Warren can no longer say "Good morning."
There was a complaint from HR about his use of it being a
micro-aggression, so he was provided with a list of alternate
greetings.

JADA: That doesn't make any sense.

SHEILA: True. But neither do any of the greetings, so it
checks out.

     (*SHEILA takes a plastic champagne flute out of her purse.*)

SHEILA: (*continuing*) I'm gonna make some coffee. Would
you like a cup?

JADA: Sure. Why are you holding a champagne flute?

SHEILA: Oh, right. You came in late yesterday. There
was a mug with an offensive saying in the break room, so there
is a list of alternate drinking cups. It's kind of fun, right? I have
another one in my purse, if you'd like one.

JADA: Um, no thanks. You can just use whatever's in
the cabinet for me.

SHEILA: Gotcha!

     (*She exits.*

     ALONSO enters wearing neckties on his knees.)

ALONSO: Good morning.

WARREN: FLARTINGA....I CAN'T! (*he runs offstage, sobbing*)

ALONSO: What's going on with him? (*pause*) Oh, that's right, last week's email. Damn, my password expires in two days, too. I better log in.

JADA: Do you have ties on your knees?

ALONSO: Yeah. They're updating the dress code in the handbook, so I'm just trying to get ahead of the curve.

JADA: Hold up. This is ridiculous. Why is everyone going along with these insane changes?

      (*SHEILA enters with her plastic champagne flute and a gas can full of coffee.*)

SHEILA: Doesn't this have the cutest straw?! It's so practical. Ooooh, it burns!

      (*DEREK enters with a sheet cake and places it on the desk. He cuts a slice and offers it to JADA.*)

DEREK: Care for a slice of Vanessa? She's casein-free!

WARREN (offstage): Casein-free...come on! We can't even dance now?!

JADA: (*shouting*) CAKE DAAAAY!

THE END

Party Planet

by **Dylan Kinnett**

Cast of Characters:

Captain, grumpy captain of a spaceship
Engineer, dutiful technician
Scientist, cynical exo-geologist
Computer, talking computer
Radio Voice, party animal on Earth

Setting:

A space ship, returning to Earth after a long, peaceful voyage to a distant planet. The inside of the spaceship contains an area where the astronauts sleep in stasis, with bed-like furnishings. There is also a command center, with the usual futuristic control panels, a porthole to see outside, and an airlock doorway.

Time:

The future.

Additional Notes:

- Scene One: The living quarters, inside the spaceship
- Scene Two: The command center, inside the spaceship
- Scene Three: Outside the spaceship
- Scene Four: The command center, inside the spaceship

We see the interior of a futuristic spacecraft. It is approaching its destination, after a long journey. The crew is waking up.

COMPUTER (offstage): All cryogenic systems have been deactivated. Raising internal temperature. Raising lights. What is your input?

ENGINEER: Captain, what are your orders?

CAPTAIN: Computer: snooze...

COMPUTER (offstage): Captain, the cryogenic systems are not equipped with snooze functionality. What is your input, Captain?

CAPTAIN: Oh. Right. Right, then. Where the hell are we?

ENGINEER: We are approaching Earth's solar system, Captain.

CAPTAIN: Ok, roll call.

ENGINEER: Chief Engineer on duty. You may take command, Captain.

CAPTAIN: Thank you. That was one hell of a nap, just now.

SCIENTIST: Chief Science Officer, reporting for duty. Hell of a nap indeed, Captain.

CAPTAIN: OK let's do a systems check and prepare to send data to Earth. Have they requested our status?

ENGINEER: Captain, they have not.

SCIENTIST: Have we heard anything else from Mission Control? I would like to know their response to the sample data we sent.

ENGINEER: We do have a transmission from them, but it's, well it's funny.

CAPTAIN: What do you mean, "it's funny"?

ENGINEER: It's, well Captain, listen to it.

(The ENGINEER calls up a recording of the last transmission from Earth. A recording of laughter plays over the intercom.

It resembles the recorded laughter used for television comedies.)

CAPTAIN: Is that the whole thing? Play the previous transmission.

(Laughter plays again.)

CAPTAIN: (*continuing*) Play the one before that.

(*More laughter.*)

CAPTAIN: (*continuing*) Where the hell are they broadcasting all this laughter from, and why?

ENGINEER: It seems to be on every single one of Earth's communication channels. What do you think it is?

SCIENTIST: You haven't been home in a while, have you? It's called hilarity television.

(*Beat. The other two are incredulous.*)

SCIENTIST: (*continuing*) It works like this: people hear fake laughter, then they laugh for real. It makes them feel better.

ENGINEER: When you hear someone else yawn, you yawn too, and you feel tired. It's like that, is it?

SCIENTIST: Oh, they have that channel, too.

(*Laughter again.*)

CAPTAIN: We're hurdling towards the Earth at top speed. This ship hasn't done any manual communicating with Mission Control in years. Landing this ship will require complex calculations and coordination with the ground base, to avoid collisions, explosions or who knows what, and all our damn radio can do is to laugh at us! Play back the earliest transmission on file. And slow this ship down!

(*More laughter plays.*)

ENGINEER: I'm sorry, Captain. Maybe there's some sort of communications malfunction.

CAPTAIN: (*to the Engineer*) I want you to suit up, get out there, and take a look at the receivers on the outside of the ship. I want to be certain we've checked everything twice. (*to the Scientist*) Take over the controls. Broadcast our position on all channels. Full stop.

   (*BLACKOUT.*)

Scene Two

During this scene, the ENGINEER is outside the ship, on a spacewalk to check the communications equipment.

The CAPTAIN and the SCIENTIST can communicate with the ENGINEER via an intercom. The outside of the ship can be represented on another part of the stage, or the ENGINEER can simply be offstage.

COMPUTER (offstage):   Airlock secure. Initiating spacewalk communications protocol.

ENGINEER (offstage):   Captain, can you read me?

CAPTAIN: Just don't do any laughing while you're out there and we'll know it's you.

ENGINEER (offstage):   No worries there, Captain. Out here, I'm nervous!

CAPTAIN: Keep your magnet boots on. We're right here on standby.

SCIENTIST: What's to be nervous about? It's just a spacewalk.

CAPTAIN: It's the new spacesuit. Probably a bit nerve-wracking to be inside that thing. It's a semi-autonomous suit.

SCIENTIST: Those suits that adjust your movements? I thought those were just prototypes.

CAPTAIN: Well, they are, but Mission Control wanted us to have one for this mission. There are only three of us up here in this very expensive can. Oxygen is precious. If the suit runs low on it, and the astronaut becomes unconscious, the suit can auto-correct, or it can be piloted from Mission Control.

SCIENTIST: That's, well, it's brilliant, I guess. They'd use our bodies as puppets?

CAPTAIN: Or, just the suits, but basically it seemed the best way to make emergency repairs and to bring the ship home.

ENGINEER (offstage):   I've made an adjustment to the equipment out here. Can you try scanning the communications channels again and see if anything has changed?

> (*SCIENTIST and CAPTAIN make adjustments. A new transmission plays. This broadcast from Earth consists of extremely upbeat music, annoyingly upbeat "catchy" or "pop" party music.*)

ENGINEER (offstage):   (*continuing*) How's that? Did it work?

> (*Beat.*)

ENGINEER (offstage): What's going on in there you guys? Are you having some kind of party? I can't hear you! What is that?

SCIENTIST: It's the transmission. It's not coming from us.

ENGINEER (offstage): Repeat. I do not copy. Over.

CAPTAIN: We are getting different signals now! Don't panic! Keep making adjustments!

ENGINEER (offstage): Copy that, Captain. This suit is making things difficult. It's like I'm arm-wrestling with myself out here.

(*The party music on the radio is interrupted.*)

SCIENTIST: Captain, I think we have an open channel!

CAPTAIN: Hailing Mission Control. Requesting Earth approach coordinates. Hailing Mission Control. Do you copy?

RADIO VOICE (offstage): Helloooo, how's everybody doing out there tonight? One, two. One, two. Testing testing. One, two. Two. Two. Two. Two. Helloooo! Mic check. Mic check. One, two. Can you hear me in the back? Can I get a whooop whoop?

CAPTAIN: Um, copy that. Requesting Earth approach coordinates. Our mission is on standby pending spaceflight directive from ground control. We're not moving until you say when.

RADIO VOICE (offstage): Yeah? Whatever! Check this out, man. I can make your ship flap its wings. Make it go flap! Flap flap flap. Fly!

ENGINEER (offstage): I'm sorry to interrupt, Captain, but my suit, it's—

RADIO VOICE (offstage): (*continuing*) Oh my god, you have got to hear this song, dude. It's the best!

(*More party music plays.*)

CAPTAIN: That racket again! What the hell is going on out there!

COMPUTER (offstage): Initiating re-entry wing deployment. Rotating re-entry wings 45 degrees. Rotating re-entry wings negative 45 degrees. Rotating re-entry wings 45 degrees. Rotating re-entry wings negative 45 degrees.

CAPTAIN: Stop it!

SCIENTIST: Captain, I can't override the commands.

ENGINEER (offstage): Captain, many of the ship's mechanical systems seem to be moving in response to the signal. I'm going to try to turn the receiver back to its original position.

CAPTAIN: Fine. And shut off that noise!

ENGINEER (offstage): I'm having trouble moving, Captain. It is very difficult to work under these conditions.

CAPTAIN: Well, I don't give a damn! Get it done. We can't just park here and listen to music all day. Let's get moving, dammit! What is going on out there? Can you see?

SCIENTIST: Well... it looks like... Dancing. There's a whole lot of dancing going on out there, Captain.

(*BLACKOUT.*)

Scene Three

Outside of the ship, the ENGINEER is doing the spacewalk.

We hear more of the music from the transmission, as well as sporadic occurrences of the canned laughter.

The ENGINEER is attempting to make adjustments to the equipment, which is perhaps similar to a satellite dish. There is zero gravity, so the ENGINEER's movements should be slow and fluid. While moving across the exterior of the ship, the space suit is receiving instructions to dance. The instructions come sporadically at first and the ENGINEER struggles to override them with other movements. After a while of this, there seems to be more dancing and less of the ENGINEER's intended movements. Eventually, the ENGINEER is overcome and the only movements are dance movements. As though it were some seductive dance move, the arms reach toward the chest of the suit, to open it revealingly.

ENGINEER: No… No… No!

        (The suit's chest is slowly pulled open. There is a terrible hissing sound as the precious oxygen escapes from the suit.

        The ENGINEER convulses briefly and dies. The suit then removes its own helmet, revealing lifeless remains within.

The suit doffs its helmet, up and down, as one might do with a hat during a tap-dance.

BLACKOUT.)

Scene Four

Inside the ship. By now, the music has reached a crescendo and shows no sign of stopping.

COMPUTER (offstage):   Exterior   airlock   opening sequence initiated.

CAPTAIN: Good! That's our engineer coming back in. When that's done, I'll shut off all the communications, even if I have to bite the wires in half with my damn teeth! I'm sick of this noise!

SCIENTIST: Captain?

CAPTAIN: What is it now?

SCIENTIST: The dancing, Captain. It hasn't stopped and, well, I thought I saw... I can't be sure what I saw. We've lost contact. I can't get any readings. Not even... Not even life support from the suit.

CAPTAIN: Never-mind all that now. It's probably just another communications malfunction acting on the suit. We'll power it down in a moment and we'll get out of here.

SCIENTIST: The outer airlock hasn't closed yet.

CAPTAIN: What?

COMPUTER (offstage):   Inner airlock opening sequence initiated.

(There is another hissing sound now, as all the air inside the ship begins to escape into the vacuum of space. The CAPTAIN and the SCIENTIST are being pulled towards the airlock as it slowly opens to reveal the ENGINEER's body standing in the doorway.)

CAPTAIN: Shut it down! Send the distress signal!

(The SCIENTIST struggles to slam on some buttons.

An alarm sounds, adding yet more sound to the crescendo of sound that has been building this whole time. The CAPTAIN and the SCIENTIST are pulled out of the ship, past the ENGINEER and into the abyss of space. The body of the ENGINEER stands ominously in the airlock doorway. Its autonomous space suit is disco dancing.)

THE END

A Scene From
Easy as Pie

by Melanie Coffey

Cast of Characters:

May Washington, (mid 20s) (she/her) - The spice,
the cyanide, driven, extreme
Natasha Spinner, (mid 20s) (she/her) - The pie crust,
solid, logical
Lou-lou Holdgate, (mid 20s) (she/her) - Sugar, butter,
cream, sweet, complacent

Setting:

Our world.

Time:

In the not so distant future.

Additional Notes:

"/" means that the next character starts speaking over the
currently speaking character.

High energy please. This doesn't have to be *West Wing* or
Gilmore Girls, but dialogue should move quickly.

SCENE: NATASHA *and* LOU-LOU *sit around the bookclub, collective space, while* MAY *paces, agitated.*

MAY: Our dear leader has signed an Executive Order restricting abortion to an extreme.

LOU-LOU: I can't believe I'm saying this, but I miss the days when the state government had some power, there were at least safe havens then.

MAY: Mm. (*a breath*) He needs to be stopped.

LOU-LOU: I'm sorry about Josh.

MAY: (*furiously*) It's fine.

LOU-LOU: Of course. You weren't even sure if you were going to say yes.

MAY: Exactly. But who the fuck breaks up with someone on the car ride back from a weekend trip? What the fuck...? But you're right, it would have been weird to be engaged. It's early.

NATASHA: It is.

MAY: It is. Plus he was a distraction.

NATASHA: Not a—

MAY: I know, I know he's life. But I find him to be...
like the trip was fun, I like camping but I'd rather be - I don't
know - volunteering at the food pantry or even signing up new
voters. I just felt bad.

LOU-LOU: Bad?

MAY: Complacent.

LOU-LOU: Oh.

MAY: Yeah. So I'm in our tent and it's cozy and
comfy and Josh is nearby making coffee and I had this idea.

NATASHA: You're going off grid?

MAY: No. (*laughs*) No. I think we should kill him.

LOU-LOU: Who? Josh?

MAY: The President.

NATASHA: What?

MAY: Yes. I think we should— I think we honestly
could. We have Rachel and Old Jeff, it wouldn't be hard to get
into an event that he attends.

LOU-LOU: But why?

MAY: Because— well there are a ton of reasons— but because Maddow is his VP. He dies, by the Constitution's orders, she becomes president.

NATASHA: Fuck.

MAY: And because of the Secret Service Strike, he has less protection now than ever before. And because he's throwing fifty percent of the population to the side and saying we have less power over our own bodies than some fucking cells.

LOU-LOU: Yeah, but—

MAY: Because the world could do with one less man who thinks his opinion on the matter counts. One less person who believes that being pro-life isn't condemning someone else. (*slight pause*) One less person that thinks pro-choice is murder instead of it being what it says it is. (*slight pause*) Because... I want Maddow now.

NATASHA: Maddow will probably run after his term.

MAY: And the damage he could do in eight years? (*beat*) People are always saying to take action. All those things on Facebook: don't just sit there and complain. And what have we been doing?

NATASHA: We go to marches and we protest.

LOU-LOU: We have this group.

MAY: (*sarcastically*) I'm loving this we. We don't do anything.

NATASHA: Okay...

MAY: You don't. When was the last time you did something for a greater cause? When was the last protest or march or riot or speech that you went to?

LOU-LOU: We're busy.

NATASHA: We're doing other things.

MAY: Ah the excuses. You've become the people we used to mock. The "oh, I don't care for politics" bullshit. What happened to you two? Hell, Nat, a few years ago you would have come to me with this plan. Now you're what? Happier keeping your head down except during election season?

NATASHA: But it's murder.

LOU-LOU: It's also murder.

MAY: Obviously. But our last presidents? I waited every day for the news of their death. First hopefully. Then desperately. And it didn't happen. Years of waiting for someone else to do it. I'm tired of waiting for other people to change the world, when I could.

NATASHA: That's fair...

MAY: (*logically*) We're not going to get a woman president. We won't. Why should future elections go any differently than they have so far? She's still never going to be as likable and approachable and as qualified and as personable as the media and men want her to be. Policies don't matter. Law degrees and Senate elections won won't ever outweigh her choice of clothes or her Late Night segments. It won't change. They like us to believe it will, but why would it?

LOU-LOU: Cautious optimism.

MAY: Is stupid. Cautious optimism means don't get your hopes up because you'll probably be heartbroken once again. No one is cautiously optimistic.

NATASHA: I know, May.

MAY: We all know. It's just a thing we say. Like 'ga'bless you' when someone sneezes even though we're not Christians.

> (*They're quiet for a moment.*)

LOU-LOU: I'm so sorry about Josh.

MAY: Don't be. I'm not even sure that I really wanted to marry him. And anyway this has nothing to do with that. It doesn't. I just want to do something. I am so tired of walking in marches that have stereos playing Britney Spears and more glitter than Pride does. I'm tired of pro-life leaders forcing their opinions on others. I'm tired of the Democratic Party capitulating and leaning to the right instead of fighting back. Fuck! You want to know why I'm going to do this? Because I threw a rock and smashed a window and suddenly whatever was constricting my lungs loosened. And for a moment I could breathe deeply and stand up straight and not feel as if I was being crushed.

> (*A beat of silence.*)

NATASHA: Let's talk about it then.

LOU-LOU: Really?

NATASHA: Yes.

(*Black out.*)

The Piece of Real Estate at the Top of the Tallest Building on Earth

by Dylan Kinnett

.

Cast of Characters:

Executive, a confident, successful executive
with an abrupt formal manner
Assistant, the fastest person in the room
Boss, the owner of the company, focused on
the big picture and cannot be bothered
with trivial details
Melvin Woodstock, a washed-up real estate investor
Barbara Witherspoon, a wealthy eccentric.

Setting:

An executive office. The furnishings are simple, sophisticated, and cutting-edge. There is a desk for the Executive and a work/reception area for the Assistant. At first it is a quiet space, but it becomes increasingly full of sound throughout the day. Broadcast news, or some other form of persistent information, should be part of the ambiance of the place at the start of the business day.

Time:

Monday morning. The near future.

"When you go in search of honey,
you must expect to be stung by bees."
— JOSEPH JOUBERT

SCENE: The EXECUTIVE enters the office and is greeted by the ASSISTANT.

ASSISTANT: Good morning!

EXECUTIVE: Good morning. What do we have today?

> (*The ASSISTANT hands some information to the EXECUTIVE.*)

ASSISTANT: You've got a sales call this morning. The boss might swing by before lunch. You have meetings scheduled at 4 p.m., 4:10, and 4:18 this afternoon...

EXECUTIVE: Wow, busy day. (*glancing at the information*) Tell the third meeting I'll be late.

ASSISTANT: You asked me to remind you to review the language for the new Altitude Initiative. It starts today and there will be an announcement.

EXECUTIVE: Where did we leave off with that?

ASSISTANT: (*points to some of the information and reads a passage*) "The changes we are making will help us to assess deliberately our buy-in, in a results oriented way. Components include rollout, gap analysis, and rejuvenated stakeholder analysis. We're making forward progress towards the mission by implementing a skill set that is both ubiquitous and bleeding-edge."

EXECUTIVE: None of that sounds even vaguely familiar. Or meaningful.

ASSISTANT: You wrote it.

EXECUTIVE: It's Monday.

(*The coffee pot makes a tone to announce that the coffee is ready.*)

ASSISTANT: Coffee?

(*The EXECUTIVE places the information on the desk and returns to retrieve the coffee.*)

EXECUTIVE: Thank you so much.

ASSISTANT: Are we buying or selling today?

EXECUTIVE: Buying, but I have a feeling there will be some selling along the way. The reports come out today. They're not good. The company needs something else to talk about today. That's why, today, we're going to buy the piece of real estate at the top of the tallest building on Earth.

ASSISTANT: So that's why they named it the Altitude Initiative.

EXECUTIVE: (*returning to desk*) Let's get started. (*sitting, preparing to make a call*) Who's first on the call schedule?

ASSISTANT: Melvin Woodstock. His property is the observation deck at the top of the Windsor Tower.

EXECUTIVE: That's his tallest building, right?

ASSISTANT: (*already listening to the phone*) Just completed, last week. I have Melvin on the line now. It's ringing. Are you ready?

EXECUTIVE: Ready... (*joining the phone conversation*) Melvin? Melvin! How are you? How's that golf game of yours?

> (*The ASSISTANT remains on the line, but is suddenly distracted by some urgent work, information, etc.*)

MELVIN (offstage):   I wish it were better, but business is way over my head lately. On top of that there's the wife, the ex-wife, the girlfriend, you know? Ha ha.

> (*The EXECUTIVE and the ASSISTANT exchange disapproving glances.*)

MELVIN: Besides, my health isn't so hot. It's gotten so bad my doctor says... Well, I can't even swing a golf club anymore.

EXECUTIVE: That's a shame, Melvin. What's the diagnosis?

MELVIN: Obesity! Look, I'm glad you called. Your boss said that you might.

(*As MELVIN talks, the ASSISTANT gestures wildly to get the EXECUTIVE to "stop," "cut, cut," or "hang up now."*)

MELVIN: I'd like to try to see if I can't interest you in a room with a view. It's a spectacular view. From up here you really can see everything. From up here, you really start to wonder how anybody could have ever thought that the world was flat.

EXECUTIVE: Yes. Impressive. Well, it seems there's a mutual interest. I'll go ahead and put something together for you to review later, okay? Bye for now!

(*The EXECUTIVE disconnects and yells to the ASSISTANT.*)

EXECUTIVE: (*continuing*) Sure, he's a cheating bastard who is too fat to swing a golf club, but we need a better reason to hang up on him than that!

ASSISTANT: (*still on the line, realizing Melvin heard the insult, trying to backtrack*) What? Oh no, no, no. That? Umm. That was "to fast for that swamp bog." There's a boat-related conversation on the other line. Ok. Alright then. We'll be in touch. Goodbye.

(*The ASSISTANT disconnects the call.*)

EXECUTIVE: He heard me.

ASSISTANT: It doesn't matter. He's no longer the owner of the piece of real estate at the top of the tallest building on Earth. That's why you needed to cut it short. They've built another one.

EXECUTIVE: Already? Wow that was fast.

(*The EXECUTIVE prepares for the call.*)

ASSISTANT: (*looking up new information*) Yes, there's a new owner, and a new piece of real estate at the top of the — Wow, that's a mouthful. Should we make an acronym?

EXECUTIVE: Yes, please. I love acronyms. But for now: who should I call?

ASSISTANT: Barbara Witherspoon on the uppermost floor of Witherspoon Tower in London. Fully furnished. Not an observation deck. This picture's nice. It's 200 meters taller than the last tower. This will be a cold call, I'm afraid. It's ringing.

EXECUTIVE: (*into the phone*) Hello, may I speak with—

BARBARA (offstage): Barbara Witherspoon, here. To be honest it's lucky you caught me. This is a brand-new number!

(*As BARBARA rambles, the ASSISTANT gestures to signal that the EXECUTIVE should end the conversation.*)

BARBARA: I travel a lot and I bought this little apartment mostly for my cat, you see. If you'd called only yesterday, it would have been just the cat at home here and nobody else but the help. How can I help you?

EXECUTIVE: (*abruptly into the phone*) Sorry, wrong number.

(*The EXECUTIVE hangs up.*)

EXECUTIVE: (*continuing, to the Assistant*) I feel like I'm prank-calling the richest people in the world.

ASSISTANT: I'm sorry about that, but Witherspoon Tower is no longer the tallest building on Earth.

EXECUTIVE: Just like that? Again? Am I getting old or is everything moving too quickly?

ASSISTANT: Yes.

EXECUTIVE: How do we get out of this mess, and on to a deal?

ASSISTANT: New deal: construction just finished on a taller one. It's in Japan. Should I get a translator?

EXECUTIVE: Don't bother. I see a trend here.

ASSISTANT: Me too. I got I.T. to install a new app. It plays a tone when there's a new piece of real estate... that meets our criteria.

(*A tone sounds to indicate when new information arrives.*)

EXECUTIVE: Seems useful.

ASSISTANT: (*seeing an ad for more software*) If you like, we can buy different tones for it. You can get things like syllables sampled from popular music!

EXECUTIVE: Just syllables?

ASSISTANT: Just syllables. Like "yeah" and "babe" and "uhh."

EXECUTIVE: Okay... Why just syllables?

ASSISTANT: Licensing fees. Attention spans? Not sure why they invented it, but people love it.

EXECUTIVE: The default is fine, I'm sure. We can tell it apart from the coffee pot. After this tone goes off, how much time will we have—

(*Tone sounds again.*)

ASSISTANT: Well it does seem to vary, but on average, I guess the interval between each opportunity is...

(*A tone sounds.*)

ASSISTANT: (*continuing*) ...increasingly shorter.

EXECUTIVE: Another idea: it takes a while to complete construction, right?

ASSISTANT: (*already working on it*) So you want another alert when construction breaks ground. Like this!

(*A second tone sounds.*)

EXECUTIVE: I was going to say: We have to hear about it, before they get started. I want an alert for the early press about it.

ASSISTANT: Like this?

(*A third tone sounds.*)

EXECUTIVE: Do we really have a need for that second tone?

(*The first tone sounds again.*)

ASSISTANT: No time for that now.

EXECUTIVE: Agreed.

(*Now there are three tones, sounding off with increasing frequency, for the remainder of the play.*

The BOSS enters, and strikes up a conversation near the ASSISTANT's work area.)

BOSS: How is everybody this morning? Good weekend? Did I hear the coffee bell in here? I've run out.

ASSISTANT: No coffee bell, but we do have coffee. It's still warm if you'd like a cup?

BOSS: Super. Use my cup. My kids got it for me. It says "the boss" on it. See? Right there. "The boss."

ASSISTANT: (*pouring a cup of coffee*) Oh I see. 'Cause you're the boss. Cute. Kids.

EXECUTIVE: Those sounds are part of a system we've got for the Altitude Initiative.

BOSS: Yes, the Altitude Initiative. We agreed to call it that, but... We did finally agree to buy the piece of real estate at the top of the tallest building on Earth?

EXECUTIVE: Yes, and we're on target. Our new system alerts us with new information about the... tall buildings.

BOSS: How much information is there?

ASSISTANT: Hear those tones?

BOSS: I thought you must have been making a whole lot of coffee in here, getting a whole lot of work done. But those tones are a lot of information?

EXECUTIVE: Yes.

BOSS: That's too much! For one lousy tower? Who cares! What, because it happens to be a few feet taller than some other tower?

ASSISTANT: Meters.

BOSS: Yes, meters. The metric system. We're behind that now. Thank you.

EXECUTIVE: It's not just that. But there's a new one every day.

BOSS: I know that, but I only care about the tallest one. Did you call Melvin?

EXECUTIVE: (*to the Assistant*) Which?

ASSISTANT: The golfer.

EXECUTIVE: No, which building. (*to the Boss*) Yes, we called Melvin.

BOSS: Super! How is Melvin? You know his health isn't so good, and I really think we're in a position to help him out.

EXECUTIVE: We were, but he's just no longer the owner of the piece of real estate at the top of the tallest building on Earth.

BOSS: Did he sell the place?

EXECUTIVE: Since the call? Maybe. We can check.

BOSS: What's the problem? I told you. No price is too high. I don't care that it's just an observation deck. We can remodel!

EXECUTIVE: There's a taller building now.

BOSS: So? We want that one! It's good enough. Lots of windows. What a view! You can look down on everybody from up there. What's the problem?

EXECUTIVE: No problem at all.

BOSS: Super. We're going forward on the partnership. Thanks for the coffee.

(*The BOSS exits.*)

EXECUTIVE: *(returning to desk)* I don't even know where to begin...

ASSISTANT: By calling Melvin?

EXECUTIVE: Oh, god. Fine.

ASSISTANT: It's ringing.

EXECUTIVE: Melvin? It's me. Returning your call. How are you?

MELVIN (offstage): How am I? I think you put it best. I'm a fat, cheating bastard, that's how I am. Why did you call?

EXECUTIVE: Well, as you know, our company is interested in the possibility of a transaction...

MELVIN: I just got off the phone selling it. To somebody else.

EXECUTIVE: Oh. I see. That's a shame. Out of curiosity though: to whom did you sell?

MELVIN: You're so clever, look it up yourself! Now excuse me. I have a doctor's appointment.

(MELVIN ends the call.)

EXECUTIVE: That went well. Who bought it?

ASSISTANT: *(looking it up)* Well, it doesn't matter because it has already re-sold and then that person already sold it to somebody else. Would you like me to set up another tone, or another phone call?

EXECUTIVE: Both please, and thank you.

ASSISTANT: It's ringing.

END OF PLAY

Love, Lust, Lyrics & Stamps

by Matt Brown
& Andre Thespies

Cast of Characters:

Summer, about twenty, sweet college girl
Mailman, middle aged, psychotic mailman
Milo, about twenty, rock star prima donna
Guard, middle aged, German guard
Crowd, an angry crowd of Germans
Award Man, hands out prizes based on merit

Setting:

Scenes take place in US and Germany during the Cold War.

Time:

The 1980s.

Additional Notes:

Originally performed with the following cast and crew:

Summer . . . . Autumn Kahl
Mailman . . . . Matt Brown
Guard . . . . Timothy Scott Craighead
Award Man . . . . David Yates

Lights & Sound . . . . Bernard B. Johnson
. . . . Chuck Green
Stage Manager . . . . Joseph Nagy
Director . . . . Tim Fitzpatrick

SCENE ONE

Scene begins with three people standing in a city street. At left is MILO, a young punk. Standing closer to stage right is SUMMER, a beautiful college girl.

Standing between them is a creepy middle aged MAILMAN. They stand still for a few moments, just staring out into the audience.

As each character speaks in an aside, they step out in front of the others. When they finish they resume their original positions.

SUMMER: The best feeling in the world is when your heart skips a beat. When you see someone that takes away every word in your mouth, leaving you breathless and searching for answers.

MAILMAN: Rain, sleet, snow or sun. You can't be afraid of dogs. Or paper cuts. Or be afraid of anthrax. Or rain, sleet, snow or sun.

SUMMER: Rain, sleet, snow or sun. Nothing could keep us apart. Then he left.

MILO: Don't get me wrong. Love is important. It's the best thing in the world to some folks.

SUMMER: Love is the best thing in the world.

MILO: I got a gig in some fancy shmancy hotel in East Germany.

MAILMAN: No room for promotions. No holiday bonus. One week of vacation. Tear down the wall.

SUMMER: If music is important to him . . . Then so be it. I love what he loves. I love his music.

MILO: Look. She's a great gal. A real firecracker. (*groan*) Smoking hot. But I'm only one man. I know this lounge act in Europe isn't worth my time or money spent on a ticket. But I need out. This is my way out.

SUMMER: He'll come back. Just wait.

MAILMAN: I need something else besides work. All I do is deliver mail. Day in and day out. At least I have Sunday off. Remember the Sabbath and keep it holy.

MILO: I'll come back. She'll wait for me here and I'll have girls waiting for me there when I come back.

SUMMER: /I'll just . . . wait.

MAILMAN: (*in unison with Summer*) I'll just . . . wait.

SCENE TWO

The MAILMAN begins delivering mail to several different houses. He greets each recipient with a smile and a simple "Hello" or "Good morning."

MAILMAN: (*aside*) You know, it's the same stuff every day. I see the same people, deliver the same letters, give the same fake greetings, same fake goodbyes. They don't care about me, no one does. They only care about their damn mail. And honestly, neither do I. They can all rot in hell for all I care. . . (*beat*) . . . Well I take that back. If they died I wouldn't have a job. (*laughs*) Seriously though, I just want to meet someone who cares. Is that too much to ask?

> (*We see SUMMER stage right. She is in her house, sitting at a table, writing a letter.*
>
> *The MAILMAN continues delivering mail, as he approaches SUMMER's house.*)

SUMMER: (*writing, aside*) To my dearest Milo . . . It has been nearly three weeks since we have been together. Often, I feel as if we are drifting apart. But then . . . But then

I remember the love that radiates from your eyes. I long for you, Milo. I feel that with each passing day, each moon and Sun, that we grow closer to being together, again. For you made me a promise. You promised me that when you return from East Germany, that you would marry me. Each night I dream. I dream of our life together, our house, our children, our love. Each night I dream and a smile comes across my face.

(*When he gets to SUMMER's house, he puts the mail in her mailbox.*

SUMMER looks up and sees the MAILMAN. She runs to the door.)

MAILMAN: Good after . . . noon, ma'am. What can I do you for?

SUMMER: I'm finishing up a letter. Can you just hold on one second?

MAILMAN: Sure thing, milady.

(*SUMMER runs inside to continue writing her letter.*)

MAILMAN: (*continuing, center stage, aside*) She's easily the most beautiful woman I've ever seen. God, I wish I had the balls to ask her out . . . But the boss says, "No flirting on the job." Ah, well she's just like everyone else. It's probably for the best. (*chuckles*) Hm. There's something wrong with her though. It's in her eyes. She's longing for something. Maybe a nice guy like me.

(*The MAILMAN returns to the mailbox and waits for SUMMER, who is writing her letter.*)

SUMMER: (*writing, aside*) Well I have to stop writing you now. The mailman's here. Write back soon! Love, Your dearest Summer.

(*SUMMER puts the letter in an envelope. She walks to the door and hands the MAILMAN her letter.*)

SUMMER: (*to the Mailman*) Here you are. So sorry for the wait!

MAILMAN: That's quite alright. So uh . . . Did you just move in? I haven't seen you around.

SUMMER: I just moved here with my boyfriend.

(*SUMMER is watering her flowers while talking.*)

MAILMAN: Oh. Where did you used to live? I can hear a southern accent on you.

SUMMER: Well haha I used to live there.

MAILMAN: Well, why did you leave? If you don't mind me asking.

SUMMER: No it's okay. We left because the prices started getting high. You know, because of the Cold War.

MAILMAN: Yeah. The Cold War sucks. I like my wars hot and spicy.

SUMMER: (*awkward laugh*) Okay. Make sure he gets that.

MAILMAN: What? You don't want to talk anymore?

SUMMER: Well I have to get back to my flowers. Plants and dirt, you know.

> (*SUMMER walks stage right to water her flowers.*
>
> *The MAILMAN stands in place and smiles at her. He then walks to center stage.*)

MAILMAN: (*aside*) Make sure he gets that? I'll do anything for you. Alright let's see where this baby is going. (*reads letter*) East Germany, here I come!

> (*The MAILMAN exits stage left.*)

SCENE THREE

The MAILMAN enters stage right and continues walking towards center stage. When he reaches center stage, he stops at a gigantic wall. The wall has the words "BERLIN WALL" written across it.
  The MAILMAN stops at the wall and studies it.

MAILMAN: When did they put this here?

      (He begins to knock on it.

      A few seconds go by as the MAILMAN waits, bewildered.

      A GUARD pops up from behind the top of the wall.)

GUARD: *(confused)* Can I help you?

MAILMAN: I need to get by!

GUARD: Alright come around back.

      (The MAILMAN walks around the wall, going upstage from the wall. After he passes the wall he walks back downstage.

      He continues walking toward stage left. MILO enters stage left.

MILO has a GIRL wrapped around his shoulder. She is kissing over his neck.

The MAILMAN walks up to MILO.)

MAILMAN: Hi, sir. Are you by any chance, Milo?

MILO: Yeah. What do you want?

MAILMAN: (*hesitating*) I have this letter here for you from a pretty girl back in the US.

MILO: Oh, okay. Great.

(MILO reads letter quickly.)

GIRL: Who's that from, baby?

MILO: Some skank from back home. Hold on a minute. (*pulls out a pen and paper, writes*) To my dearest Summer, It has been nearly three weeks since we've had sex. Hugs and kisses, Milo. (*passes the letter to the Mailman*) Give this to her. Would ya'?

(MILO hands the MAILMAN the letter he just wrote. He then moves farther stage left. He discards SUMMER's letter in a nearby trashcan and exits stage left.

The MAILMAN walks over to the trashcan, he pulls out the letter, and he reads it.)

MAILMAN: (*reading the letter*) "To my dearest Milo, It has been nearly three weeks since we have been together . . ." (*beat*) Oh Summer . . . your words are so kind and soft and pretty and beautiful. Milo's eyes aren't deserving enough to read words as pure as yours. Every syllable sends chills down my spine. Every sentence makes me warm inside. Every period—well a period is just punctuation. The punctuation doesn't do much for me. (*gets back to reading the letter*) "Often I feel we are drifting apart." Yes! Yes. This is finally my chance. (*back to the letter*) "But then I remember the love that radiates from your eyes . . ." (*crumples the letter a little*) Love? What love? I've seen Milo. Now I know his eyes aren't capable of love. Nothing that grotesque and shallow and still can be capable of loving a girl as beautiful as Summer. (*growing louder*) I've got to tell her. She has to know. (*even louder, violent*) I've got to tell her! She has to know!

(*The MAILMAN walks back to the wall.*)

MAILMAN: (*screaming*) Move this wall! (*pounds fist on wall*)

(*The GUARD pops up from the top of the wall.*)

GUARD: (*same tone as before*) How can I help you?

MAILMAN: I need to get by.

GUARD: Alright, come around back.

MAILMAN: (*screaming*) You don't deserve a nice girl like Summer.

GUARD: (*chuckling, confused*) What are you talking about?

MAILMAN: (*screaming*) GAHHHH!

(*The MAILMAN pulls off his shoe and throws it at the GUARD. The GUARD yells in pain and falls from his post. The MAILMAN kicks the wall over on top of the GUARD.*)

A REVOLUTIONARY enters stage left.)

REVOLUTIONARY: Yeah! Tear down that wall!

(*The MAILMAN walks upstage around the wall and exits stage right.*

As the MAILMAN leaves, a huge crowd of people enters stage left.

The crowd surrounds the wall from the left side and begin pushing on the wall.)

SCENE FOUR

The scene opens with the MAILMAN engaged in conversation with SUMMER at her house at stage right.

SUMMER: (*in tears*) What are you talking about? Why would you say these things?

MAILMAN: (*pacing, shouting*) He doesn't deserve you! He doesn't deserve! (*beat*) I deserve you! I deserve you!

SUMMER: Get away from me! I don't believe any of this!

MAILMAN: (*grabs her, screams*) Listen to me! You're just like the rest of them! Just like the rest!

SUMMER: (*pulls away*) You'd better stop . . . (*sobbing*) My boyfriend's flight is due back any minute now!

MAILMAN: Good I have to have a little chit-chat with him. (*maniacal laughter*)

(*The MAILMAN paces back and forth by SUMMER's house, talking to himself.*

SUMMER goes inside her house, she locks the door, and she sits on her couch to cry.

The MAILMAN paces back and forth, looking more insane with each pass.

MILO enters stage left and approaches the MAILMAN.)

MAILMAN: (*to Milo*) There you are!

MILO: Who are you again?

(*The MAILMAN pulls a pistol out of his mail sack.*)

MILO: (*continuing*) What, do I owe you money?

MAILMAN: You took her from me! This is all your
fault!

MILO: What, are you crazy?

MAILMAN: Crazy in love!

(*MILO pulls out his own gun, from the back of his pants.*

An AWARD MAN, in a suit, enters stage left. He is holding a letter in his hand. He casually walks up to the MAILMAN and stares at him.

Unbeknownst to the MAILMAN, SUMMER is standing right by him, watching the remainder of the scene.)

AWARD MAN: Are you Clark McFiniggan?

MAILMAN: (*confused*) Yes.

174

AWARD MAN: Clark McFiniggan, a mailman?

MAILMAN: Not a mailman, the mailman.

AWARD MAN: Well, you've been awarded the Nobel Peace Prize for your efforts in East Germany. Congratulations.

> (*The MAILMAN reaches for the letter, as MILO shoots him.*
>
> *The AWARD MAN shrugs and hands the prize to MILO. He casually exits stage left.*
>
> *MILO walks over to SUMMER. They hug.*
>
> *GIRL enters stage left.*)

GIRL: Lover!

> (*MILO turns and shoots GIRL, she dies.*
>
> *MILO turns to SUMMER and shrugs. They hug.*)

THE END

Starry Night

by John Joseph Enright

Cast of Characters:

Isabella, 20s to 30s
Visitor, any age
William, 20s to 30s

Setting:

Under an open sky.

Time:

Tomorrow night.

SCENE: *Campsite. Night.*
  ISABELLA *looks up at the sky.*

ISABELLA: I mean, look at all those
stars, William. Stars with planets. What are the odds? There has
to be life on some of those planets. William? Are you awake?

VOICE FROM THE DARK: I am awake.

ISABELLA: What the — who is that?

VOICE FROM THE DARK: We are just visiting.

ISABELLA: William!

WILLIAM: I'm asleep.

ISABELLA: Well wake up!

          (*VISITOR steps into light. He has antennas on his head.*)

VISITOR: You are the one we wish
to speak with. Not him.

ISABELLA: Why are you wearing antennas on your head?

VISITOR: I am not wearing antennas.

ISABELLA: I can see them.

VISITOR: Your eyes are functioning correctly. But your brain is making an incorrect inference.

WILLIAM: Honey, who is this guy?

ISABELLA: I have no idea.

WILLIAM: Listen, buddy.

VISITOR: I am not your buddy, and I have no particular interest in listening to you at this time.

ISABELLA: Wait. What incorrect inference?

WILLIAM: Is this one of your professor friends?

VISITOR: I am not wearing antennas. They are part of me.

WILLIAM: Do you know this guy, or not?

ISABELLA: Be quiet.

WILLIAM: Quiet?

ISABELLA: Show me.

WILLIAM: Show you?

ISABELLA: Not you. Him. Show me. Let me feel your antenna.

VISITOR: This is a very rude request.

ISABELLA: You are making an extraordinary claim.

VISITOR: I suppose there are parts of your body that you would not want me to touch.

WILLIAM: You bet there are.

VISITOR: You grew up without antennas. You do not understand. I forgive you.

ISABELLA: William?

WILLIAM: Yes?

ISABELLA: That pot we smoked. Where did you get it?

WILLIAM: From the dispensary.

ISABELLA: Not from the street?

WILLIAM: No.

ISABELLA: Nothing added to it.

WILLIAM: Of course not.

ISABELLA: So this is happening.

WILLIAM: If someone took something illegal, I'd say it was him.

VISITOR: Your cannabis has no effect on my species.

WILLIAM: Your species?

VISITOR: And in any event, I am not concerned with your laws.

ISABELLA: Whether you are concerned with our laws or not, they are concerned with you. And you are trespassing on our campsite.

VISITOR: You are Isabella Jeanette Halvorsen?

ISABELLA: How do you know that?

VISITOR: Author of the paper, Xeno-Biology, How To Recognize An Alien?

ISABELLA: Well, co-author.

VISITOR: You did most of the writing, did you not?

ISABELLA: Yes. But. No.

VISITOR: No?

ISABELLA: You're not claiming to be?

VISITOR: How do you do, Isabella. I am a visitor to your planet.

ISABELLA: Who put you up to this?

VISITOR: I have been sent by our highest authority.

ISABELLA: No. I mean. You're really good at this. Do you like, do improv?

VISITOR: Improv. Improv. Checking reference. Ah. An alleged art form involving spontaneous impersonation. No. I have never tried that. It is not something our people prize.

ISABELLA: That's good. Very good. Leo put you up to this, right? He has all sorts of actor friends.

VISITOR: This has nothing to do with your friend, Leo. I am here to make first contact. With you.

ISABELLA: Me? Why me? Shouldn't you start with the President?

VISITOR: I tried that. It did not go well.

ISABELLA: Oh.

VISITOR: The President was upset. His guardians were upset. I had to wipe their memories.

ISABELLA: You can wipe memories?

VISITOR: About twenty minute's worth. It's not safe to go back further. Brain damage may occur.

ISABELLA: Well, prove it.

VISITOR: Prove it?

ISABELLA: Show me.

VISITOR: If I wipe your memory, I will prove nothing to you, because you will not remember making the request.

ISABELLA: Damn you're good. Wait. Okay. Then do it to William.

WILLIAM: What?

ISABELLA: Honey. There are no such things as memory wipes. I'm just proving a point. He's gone too far with this story. He'll make some excuse now. About how it's unethical to wipe your memory.

> (*VISITOR hits button on some device.*
>
> *WILLIAM falls asleep.*)

VISITOR: It is done.

ISABELLA: William!

WILLIAM: (*waking*) What is it?

ISABELLA: Quit it!

WILLIAM: Quit what?

VISITOR: See?

WILLIAM: Who is this guy?

ISABELLA: William, quit playing.

WILLIAM: Playing what?

VISITOR: William, you've never seen me before, have you?

WILLIAM: I think I'd remember those antennas.

VISITOR: That's right. You would. They are quite distinctive. And, if I do say so myself, they are a particularly fine pair.

WILLIAM: Why are you wearing them?

VISITOR: Well, as it turns out, I'm a visitor from another planet, and these antennas are part of my body.

WILLIAM: Isabella. Is this your idea of a gag?

ISABELLA: No.

VISITOR: Our experience with your President made it clear to us that we do not yet understand your social structure. Instead of starting at the top of your power pyramid, we decided to start at the top of your knowledge pyramid. In this case, it is you.

ISABELLA: I'm only a graduate student.

VISITOR: Nonetheless, we have researched your planet's academic literature on dealing with aliens, and we found your paper to be the most sensible. It has many wrong ideas, of course. But it is better than the rest.

ISABELLA: You think so?

VISITOR: We know so. Our plan is to strategize with you about next steps.

WILLIAM: Next steps?

VISITOR: We wish to establish a small station upon this planet. So that we may visit you and study you. But we wish to do so under peaceful terms. We do not wish to be attacked by your crude nuclear weapons.

ISABELLA: You don't have defenses against nukes?

VISITOR: We do. But it would be bad for your environment.

ISABELLA: You've got this all worked out, don't you?

VISITOR: You have credibility with more senior researchers in Xeno-biology. We hope that you will be able to introduce us to them. We hope that your top scientists will be able to secure us a more favorable second interview with your President.

ISABELLA: Well, it sounds like a plan. But, you know, all the senior scientists are asleep now. It would be rude to call them all together now. Why don't you come back in the morning?

WILLIAM: You're not buying this, are you?

ISABELLA: Sh.

WILLIAM: Oh. You just want him to go away.

ISABELLA: Sh.

VISITOR: We thought it was better to approach you when

your hemisphere of the planet was dark. So we would not cause a disturbance.

ISABELLA: Yes. That was a great idea. And it worked, right? You have made contact. And I believe you completely. And I will help you reach out to top scientists and the President. But let's do all that tomorrow, all right? I need my sleep now.

VISITOR: You just want me to go away.

ISABELLA: Yes.

VISITOR: You do not believe me.

ISABELLA: No. But it's not your fault. You were excellent.

VISITOR: Thank you.

WILLIAM: Now you need to go.

VISITOR: A moment more of your time, if I may.

WILLIAM: No. Now.

(*WILLIAM brandishes camp shovel at VISITOR.*

VISITOR presses button. WILLIAM falls to ground, asleep.)

ISABELLA: So William's in on this.

VISITOR: That's right. William is part of our humorous deception. But now it is time for a debrief. Tell me what things

I did wrong. You are a person who believes in the possibility of alien life. Why did you not believe in me?

ISABELLA: Well, to start with, those antennas are a bit much.

VISITOR: Really? I see. What else?

ISABELLA: Well, maybe instead of just announcing yourself, you could begin by giving me some fake scientific information about the biology of your world. Something plausible, to intrigue me.

VISITOR: So, perhaps some technical description of how our XNA is different than your DNA.

ISABELLA: Exactly. Wow. You really researched this.

VISITOR: What else should I have done differently?

ISABELLA: Also, maybe you could have begun by apologizing for the intrusion? We're out here in the middle of nowhere in the dark. Normal human beings don't just walk up on each other and start talking. Unless they're in need of help.

VISITOR: But. The role I am playing. I am not a normal human being.

ISABELLA: Listen. You seem like a nice enough guy. And this was a funny bit. But you startled me the way you came up.

VISITOR: Ah. I made you feel defensive.

ISABELLA: Yes.

VISITOR: And so you were less inclined to believe what I was saying.

ISABELLA: That's right.

VISITOR: I see. Thank you. Have a nice sleep. It is a clear night. Very favorable for stargazing.

ISABELLA: Yes.

VISITOR: Do you see that tiny yellow star, just to the left of Arcturus?

ISABELLA: What about it?

VISITOR: Nothing. Have a nice nap.

> (*ISABELLA looks at the VISITOR.*
>
> *WILLIAM wakes up.*)

WILLIAM: Who is this guy?

> (*VISITOR hits a button. ISABELLA and WILLIAM fall asleep.*
>
> *VISITOR takes a blanket and wraps it like a turban over his head, covering his antennas from view.*
>
> *VISITOR hits a button, takes a step back.*
>
> *ISABELLA wakes.*)

ISABELLA: Is someone there?

(*VISITOR steps forward.*)

VISITOR: Excuse me. I am terribly sorry to intrude. But I need help.

ISABELLA: What kind of help? William. Wake up.

VISITOR: It has to do with XNA.

ISABELLA: What about it?

VISITOR: I have evidence that actual life forms can be constructed by peptide nucleic acid.

ISABELLA: How?

WILLIAM: Who is this?

ISABELLA: I don't know, but he's speaking my language.

VISITOR: I am merely a visitor, seeking help.

(*Blackout.*)

END OF PLAY.

Biographical Information

MATT BROWN (*Love, Lust, Lyrics & Stamps*) lives in Sykesville, Maryland with his family and son. He co-wrote this play as part of an original theatrical showcase. Matt has written sketches and scenes for musicals and plays. He enjoys writing in a collaborative atmosphere, and he's always coming up with fresh ideas to inspire his writing partners. Brown had his debut performance as the Mailman in *Love, Lust, Lyrics & Stamps*.

BARBARA BRYAN (*Leaving the Universe*) is a Baltimore playwright whose work has been performed at theaters across the US. Her plays have been finalists for the O'Neill National Playwrights Conference, PlayLabs, and the Heideman Award from Actors Theatre of Louisville. Barbara received grants from Baltimore City Arts, Maryland State Arts Council, and Creative Baltimore. She participated in the Kennedy Center Summer Playwriting Intensive and has developed plays in Paul Berman's Theater Workshop in Baltimore. Bryan is a graduate of Trinity College, Washington, DC.

MELANIE COFFEY (*To You & Me & the Ocean, Easy as Pie*) is a screenwriter, filmmaker, and playwright. Growing up on the Connecticut coast and earning an Honors BFA in Film in New York, Melanie currently resides in Chicago, where she recently earned her MFA in Writing for the Screen and Stage from Northwestern University. Coffey is a member of the Chicago Dramatists Guild and the Playwrights' Center, and her work in theater, television, and film has been performed, read, and/or screened in New York City, Chicago, San Diego, Los Angeles, Mystic (Connecticut), Edinburgh (Scotland), and London (England).

JOHN JOSEPH ENRIGHT (*Iago's Deal, Starry Night*) is a playwright and poet from the South Side of Chicago, best known for his full-length romantic comedies and short science-fiction plays. John's plays are usually first produced in Chicago, which has an energetic theater scene, but he is always happy when something he wrote receives a production elsewhere. His romantic comedy, *O'Brien & O'Brian*, was featured in the 2015 New York International Fringe Festival. His short play, *Kitties in Space*, was featured in the 2019 Science Fiction Theatre Festival in London.

On the poetry side of things, John is the author of *Starbound And Other Poems*, and he is known on the internet for his "rhyme of the day" posts, which are mostly humorous observations based on current events and doings. He is currently working with composer Anne Tan on *Charmin: The Musical*, a short comedy about the great bathroom tissue shortage of 2020. Enright also enjoys acting and feels that the experience of performing on stage helps him to write pieces that allow actors to reach out to an audience.

DYLAN KINNETT (*Party Planet, The Piece of Real Estate at the Top of the Tallest Building on Earth*) is a writer, spoken word performance artist, and the founding editor of *Infinity's Kitchen*. His work blends literary practice with new media, hypertext, and theater. Kinnett holds a BA in Writing from Maryville College in Tennessee and has work published or performed by Annex Theater at Artscape, Cambridge Community Television, The University of Baltimore, and Les Kurbas Theatre in Ukraine. Dylan lives in Baltimore, Maryland.

EMMA S. RUND (*To Fix A Dinosaur*) is a Chicago-based playwright, baker, and avid reader. On an average rainy day, you can find Emma fulfilling the writer stereotype by either reading or writing, while drinking something hot, in a turtleneck sweater. Perhaps she's even munching on a fresh batch of chocolate chip cookies.

Graduating from college in 2019, Emma moved to Chicago to join the real theatre world, and she has been adapting to the world of virtual theatre. Emma is passionate about stories centering on womxn. "There are not enough complicated womxn onstage, and we deserve to be seen in all our wonderful complexity. We also deserve to be seen in all our diversity. Feminism must be intersectional and putting more white women onstage is not good enough," says Rund.

Since Emma began writing, she has had the pleasure of workshopping her plays with companies like Chicago Dramatists, Women's Theatre Alliance, Playpenn, The Playground Experiment, and Digital Dramatists. Emma's 10-minute play, *To Fix A Dinosaur*, has had recognition as a winner of The Hive Collaborative's 10-minute play competition, and this play was featured in an episode on the Ensemble Theatre of Chattanooga's 'Lights Up!' podcast. Emma's full-length plays, *Personal Library*, *Rosemary & Time*, and *The Bushwick Girls*, have been developed at DePaul University, Ball State University, and with Women's Theatre Alliance, respectively.

ALEXANDER SCALLY (*Cake Day, Chalked*) is a Baltimore-based theatre artist whose plays and performance work have been featured in Baltimore, Washington (DC), Philadelphia, and New York City. Scally is a founding member of Glass Mind Theatre (2009-2015) and current member of the Submersive Collective, a group of artists who devise original, immersive theatre experiences in historical landscapes.

Alexander's self-produced one-act plays include *Spam Filter* and *Apply Within*, which premiered in his multimedia series, 'Fragments'. *Apply Within* was remounted in 2014 for the free arts festival, Scapescape. Two other short plays, *In Transit* and *RSVP (Robert, Sandra, Vicki, Paul)*, were produced and published with BOOM Theatre in their annual Brave New Works festival.

Alexander's work was featured in Charm City Fringe Festival, including his solo performance piece, *BUILDING YOUR EMOTIONAL HOME with DAVID MARK DAVIDS*, and original sketch comedy project, *URBAN SPRAWL*. Both of these pieces were created and produced with Alexander's wife, Caitlin Bouxsein, under BOUXSCAL Productions.

CAMERON SHEPPARD (*Mary Doesn't Wear Red Lipstick*) is a Chicago-based writer and actor. She has been honing her skills in playwriting over the past few years. Her works (including *Mary Doesn't Wear Red Lipstick*, *As She Drowns*, and

Other Sides) have been developed and presented in conjunction with Women's Theatre Alliance of Chicago and Loyola University Chicago, where she will receive her Bachelor's in English in May.

Drawing on her experiences as a young queer woman, Cameron seeks to expose complex narratives that are often overlooked. Her plays engage with subjects of faith, LGBTQ+ issues, abortion, identity, addiction, and the erasure of women's stories throughout history. In her spare time, Sheppard can be found testing new stand-up material at local open mics or exploring the great outdoors with her dog, Henry.

ANDRE THESPIES (*Love, Lust, Lyrics & Stamps*) started as an actor, but he quit acting when he suffered severe injuries and back pain. Andre started writing poetry to deal with his misfortune. He soon found a better way for his words to reach the stage, producing his first original play at a community theatre in the Mid-Atlantic region.

Andre collaborated with Matt Brown to create *Love, Lust, Lyrics & Stamps* as an opening play to accompany his science fiction debut, *Boy Meets Bot*. This full-length piece finds its place as the second part of a science fiction, literary series called *Our Robotic Future*. Andre penned a musical called *Animalul din Interior* and other works for stages in Chicago, Boston, and Seattle, but he wasn't fulfilled with the depth of his work in those early years.

Andre took time from the theatre prior to taking up endeavors of writing for social change, as exemplified in *A Tale Continued*. This play focuses on the legacy of Aesop, a legendary slave who turned wit upon his master. Thespies writes about his ancestors, and he's obsessively looking for ways to improve his comprehension of the depths of the human spirit.

SHAUN VAIN (Editor) is responsible for *The Lost Poetry* and a handful of novels. As a novelist, he enjoys exploring genre, including the noir detective story, the fable, and science fiction. Although Shaun obtained formal training in writing and scholarly research, he often relishes in mysterious, imaginative meanderings.

While traveling and appreciating the splendors of the world, Shaun gathers a thoughtful blend of characters, stories, and themes. In his free time, Vain enjoys cycling, nature, and conversations with interesting people.

Performance Rights

All of the plays included in this anthology are protected by copyright laws of the United States. To obtain permission to perform *To You & Me & the Ocean*; *Leaving the Universe*; *Mary Doesn't Wear Red Lipstick*; *To Fix A Dinosaur*; *Chalked*; *Cake Day*; *Easy as Pie*; *Love, Lust, Lyrics & Stamps*, you must contact the publisher, or contact the playwright (their estate, agent, or manager).

COPYRIGHT EXCEPTIONS

Reproduction of this anthology and/or public performance in any fashion is prohibited, apart from the exceptions made in this notice. The following plays may be performed without prior written notice, only if credit is given to the author(s): *Iago's Deal*, *Party Planet*, *The Piece of Real Estate at the Top of the Tallest Building on Earth*, *Starry Night*.

PRODUCING NEW WORK

One of the main goals of publishing an anthology of plays is to promote the production of new work, so Future Publishing House will make every effort to assist, as a liaison, in providing rights to perform these works.

FOR CLASSROOM SETTINGS

If plays, monologues, or scenes from plays are performed in a classroom setting without the use of recording devices, there is no need to contact the publisher or playwrights. However, we take pride in our work, so we love to hear of such activities.

Index

Lightning Source UK Ltd.
Milton Keynes UK
UKHW011100060121
376497UK00011B/445/J